HOME AND SMALL BUSINESS GUIDE TO PROTECTING YOUR COMPUTER NETWORK, ELECTRONIC ASSETS, AND PRIVACY

HOME AND SMALL BUSINESS GUIDE TO PROTECTING YOUR COMPUTER NETWORK, ELECTRONIC ASSETS, AND PRIVACY

Philip Alexander

Westport, Connecticut
London

Library of Congress Cataloging-in-Publication Data

Alexander, Philip, 1963–
   Home and small business guide to protecting your computer network, electronic assets, and privacy /
   Philip Alexander.
     p. cm.
   Includes bibliographical references and index.
   ISBN 978–0–313–36007–7 (alk. paper)
1. Small business—Computer networks—Security measures. 2. Small business—Data processing—
Security measures. 3. Computer networks—Security measures. 4. Computer security. 5. Database
security. I. Title.
HF5548.37.A438 2009
005.8—dc22   2008046773

British Library Cataloguing in Publication Data is available.

Library of Congress Catalog Card Number: 2008046773
ISBN: 978–0–313–36007–7

First published in 2009

Praeger Publishers, 88 Post Road West, Westport, CT 06881
An imprint of Greenwood Publishing Group, Inc.
www.praeger.com

Printed in the United States of America

The paper used in this book complies with the
Permanent Paper Standard issued by the National
Information Standards Organization (Z39.48-1984).

10 9 8 7 6 5 4 3 2 1

CONTENTS

PREFACE

They're out there: data security books, written to make computer systems harder to hack. Most are written in that secret language known only to computer engineers. I've heard terms, including *techno-babble* and *engineer-ese* to describe how engineers appear to speak in tongues when overheard by non-computer-savvy people. That certainly applies to books like these—but not this one. There are also myriad resources for people trying to obtain any one of the dozens of data security certifications available in the industry today. These books are all well and good; but then again they are geared towards either the computer engineer or the information security professional, not to the general public. I must plead guilty, as I have also written books and articles for that audience.

It's time for a book on data security that the average computer user can understand. I've seen it time and again: people get frustrated because they don't know if their computers are secure or even working properly. Most people, for example, want to keep the personal information stored on computers safe. They know the hackers are out there but aren't sure how best to protect themselves, their computers, and the data stored therein. The problem is that to many, the computer is such a mystical black box, that they don't even know where to start or what questions to ask. In frustration, some chose to go to the non-techno extreme, and live "off the grid" so to speak. They don't have e-mail accounts, and they don't surf the Web for fear of being hacked. They might not even use credit or debit cards to reduce the risk of identity theft. While these measures certainly will work to a point, they are not the silver bullet one might think they are. Whenever we go see a doctor, get a prescription filled, obtain a driver's license, or apply for a job, we give people information about us. Information that, if not properly safeguarded, could expose us to the risks of identity theft. In some cases, there's not much we can do. But a variety of simple steps, which this book describes, can increase the security of our home or small business computer systems manifold.

I've also been heartbroken when I learn of a friend who has been taken advantage of by unscrupulous salespeople tricking them into buying far more equipment and software than is necessary in order to make full use of their home and small business computers. While I have long been instinctively aware of the need for a comprehensive resource for the non-computer geeks out there, it never dawned on me to write a book on the topic. Until now.

It has often been said that some of our best inspirations come from having discussions with our friends. Well, in this case, it is certainly true, for it was while discussing with a couple of my friends the release of my second book, *Information Security: A Manager's Guide to Thwarting Data Thieves and Hackers,* that we touched on the need for a similar guide for average users. Soon thereafter, I was asked to consider writing a data security book for the general public, one geared to small businesses as well as owners of home computers. In other words, a data security book for the rest of us.

This book contains straight talk for those concerned with safe practices for everyday computer usage as well as data security issues. I'll talk about ways to protect your small business computers and electronic data. Arguably, small businesses can be at a greater risk if their computer systems are lost, since they often don't have elaborate backup plans like big businesses do.

I will also discuss tips and tricks on how to protect home computers, whether for personal use or for that home-based business. I've provided some guidelines on how to safeguard your personal information when purchasing items online. As a parent, I'm also keenly aware that the Internet can be an incredible wealth of information. My two sons regularly use it to help with their schoolwork. However, the Internet can, unfortunately, also be a very dangerous place, frequented by—or perhaps I should say infested with—child predators. So, as one parent to another, I've included some tips on how to help protect our children. Because cell phones, PDAs, and other mobile electronic devices have security issues as well, I will discuss methods for keeping data safe and secure. Tips and tricks on how not to become a victim of identity theft? You bet—that's in here too.

Most importantly, I cover ways to keep our kids safe while they're surfing the Internet. Whether it's cyberbullying, online predators, or just plain "stranger danger," the Internet can be as dangerous as it is informative.

Here is my promise to you: You will find no strange computer jargon that goes into elaborate discussions about, for instance, the differences between any-cast and broad-cast network traffic. I'll keep out of this book any of the vernacular spoken amongst computer security professionals but not commonly used by the general public. Bottom line: You'll get plain-English, non-techie advice on how to keep your computers running and your data safe in this high-tech world that we live in.

We have a lot of ground to cover, so let's get started.

ACKNOWLEDGMENTS

As I'm finalizing what is now my third book, I must admit to still experiencing a certain degree of disbelief. If anybody would have told me 10 years ago that I would be a published author, I would have laughed. Then, while sitting at a presentation discussing the current state of data security compliance, the idea for my first book came to me. What is now what I realize to be reverse order—I wrote the book first, and then tried to find a company that would agree to publish it. I have also learned that if you thrive on rejection, try to become a published author. Of the more than a dozen publishing companies that I approached, most didn't even acknowledge me. The rest all turned me down, except for one, of course. As the saying goes, lightning only needs to strike once to get lucky, and hence my first book, *Data Breach Disclosure Laws—A State-by-state Perspective* was born. The experience also told me to follow your dreams. You will never know what you are capable of if you don't try. If you have a dream a writing a book yourself, go for it.

This leads me into wanting to acknowledge the publisher of my next two books, Greenwood Publishing Group, and especially my editor Jeff Olson. Jeff was one of the editors that I reached out to trying to pitch my first book. Jeff contacted me and asked if I could write a book on information security at a broader level, targeting compliance officers, senior executives, information security officers as well as risk officers. Almost a year later my second book, *Information Security: A Manager's Guide to Thwarting Data Thieves and Hackers* hit the bookshelves. Now fully into the groove of writing, I had an idea to write a computer security book aimed at helping the general public. I pitched the idea to Jeff, and lo and behold, here we are with what is now my third book. So, I want to extend a personal thank you to Jeff for working with me.

I also want to acknowledge both my Uncle Max and Aunt Myrna. I believe that every boy needs a strong male figure to help guide him through the journey of life and make the transition from childhood to becoming a man. If you're lucky, that person will be your father. It was my father for me until he passed away when I was 25 years old. While no person could ever replace my dad in my heart, my Uncle Max has been like a second father to me, always there to offer the fatherly advice that I have come to value so much even into my forties. Thanks, Uncle Max—you're the best. My Aunt Myrna has always been there for me was well. She is always supportive, and the high opinion that she has of me is humbling. I only hope that I can be the person that my Aunt Myrna believes that I am.

I also want to thank my wife Cency and our two sons Freddy and Danny. Writing a book takes a lot of time and energy. It's time and energy that was not spent on them. While I always tried my best to take time out to be the good husband and father, I must acknowledge their sacrifices, as well. I spent long hours conducting research and writing the formation of this book. It's time that I didn't spend with them. So, to quote a line that many professional athletes have used in the past, "Pack your bags kids, we're off to Disneyland."

Chapter 1

JOB #1: SECURE YOUR NETWORK

Experts in the field of computer data security often state, and correctly so, that there are no silver bullets when it comes to securing a computer network. No one piece of hardware or software exists that will secure your computer and the data contained in it, from all evils that can possibly affect it. This would include things such as malware—a fancy word for computer viruses as well as other kinds of malicious software—and, of course, attacks from hackers. For medium-to-large companies with expansive computer networks, that statement is absolutely true.

However, in this case, I'm not talking about large computer networks. The focus of this book is centered on securing computer systems of a much smaller scale. This could mean a small business, a home-based business, or even the computers in your house. These computing systems are mainly used for e-mailing, surfing the Web, storing the pictures that you've taken with your digital camera, and performing research for a school project.

Securing a small computer network is akin to locking all the doors and windows in your house. Once done, a certain degree of security has, in fact, been obtained. Conversely, trying to lock all the doors and windows in every house and every business in a large city such as Chicago or New York would be incredibly difficult. Just as there are fewer doors and windows to lock in a single house, it is also easier to secure the computers that are just used either by your immediate family or by a handful of employees, than it is to secure a network used by tens of thousands of employees in a large company.

HACKERS AND WHY THEY HACK

Hackers are motivated by different things. It's akin to asking why people commit arson. Some do it to try to collect on the insurance money, while others have a mental disorder that compels them to commit arson. Then, there are others that burn down homes out of a sense of social justice if the structure is built in an area that they believe should be left undeveloped.

Whatever the motivation, the end result of an arsonist is the same: fire damage to various degrees. The same is true with hackers. While their motivations may differ, the end results of hacking are generally the same. Your computer doesn't work as it should, your data is stolen—or in some cases, it's a combination of both. Large companies are often the specific target of hackers. A company may be involved in a business that is politically divisive and that invites the ire of people who don't share the same view. Potential hackers could deem the company to be either socially or environmentally irresponsible. Whatever the reason that the perpetrator uses to justify the activity, the act of being a hacker activist has been labeled "Hacktivism." Hacktivists are comparable to the aforementioned arsonists that burn down homes built in places that they feel should be left undeveloped.

Sometimes hackers target businesses due to the nature of the data that they collect. Businesses that accept credit cards as payment for their products and services are often the target of those trying to steal information in order to commit financial fraud. Just having personally identifiable information, such as Social Security numbers, on a network will attract hackers intent on committing identity theft.

Sometimes, the only reason a hacker will choose a target comes down to simple bragging rights. This is the hacker who is looking for the right to be able to post the fact that they just hacked a famous company's computer network on a hacking community Web site.

While home computers and small business computing networks certainly pose less of a target, they certainly are not risk free. Whether it's a novice hacker trying to better hone his skills, or a more seasoned one wanting to take over your systems for some nefarious purpose, small networks are at risk from hackers as well.

LIMIT PHYSICAL ACCESS TO YOUR COMPUTERS

Large companies take elaborate measures to control the physical access to their servers. It is not uncommon to have entire buildings specifically designed to house servers and, as such, to contain a huge number of physical security controls. Such buildings are referred to as data centers. A common security measure is the presence of an around-the-clock uniformed security guard, on site 24 hours a day, 7 days a week. In addition, employees are generally required to display a special photo identification badge at all times. Often, that badge has data imprinted on it, in a fashion similar to the magnetic strip on a credit card. The data will let them gain access to certain areas of the data center, while denying access to other areas. The badge may also limit the times when an employee can access the building. The heart of the data center itself may very well require some sort of biometric authentication such as a fingerprint in order to gain entry. Even if an employee can get into the same room with the servers, the servers will be in locked cages. To be able to actually get to the servers themselves, the employee has to be authorized not only to be in the server room, but also to be able to check out a key to a particular cage containing the servers he is trying to access. On top of that security, it is common for server rooms to also be equipped with closed-circuit television cameras, which monitor the entire building and record his every move.

While a small business with a handful of employees is not going to have a dedicated data center, controlling physical access to the computers that you use for your small business is very important. If you allow a hacker physical access to a server, the question becomes not whether or not they will be able to break into the system, but when. The same goes for workstations and laptops. There are steps that can be taken that are neither as grandiose nor as expensive as the aforementioned data centers. Placing your computers in a locked office at your place of business is a more secure solution than putting them in an area that is frequented by customers or delivery people. Consider your computers to be sensitive equipment, and try to limit their exposure to the general public. If your employees' job descriptions do not require the use of a computer, don't leave your business's computers where employees could access them. Treat your computers as you would treat your employees' personnel files.

There is also something to be said for the concept of "security by obscurity," similar to the concept of *out of sight, out of mind.* Just by keeping your computer out of plain sight, you will reduce the chance that somebody will try to "tinker" with it. Instead of placing it in a highly trafficked area in your place of business, keep it in your office. Put your computer in a place where only those with a legitimate need to access it can. Employees with no business need to sit at the desk in your office are less likely to mess with your computer that is in there as well. Locking your office door when you leave will not only help protect your computer, but also other items that you have in there. That includes business plans, personnel files, customer lists, invoices, and anything else that you wouldn't want your employees to see.

Over the span of my career (20 years and counting), I have seen computers located in some crazy places. I have seen brand-new computers, still in their boxes, propping open doors in desolate areas in the dead of night. That is almost like sending out an invitation to steal them. When I expressed my concern, I was told that since there was no data on the computers yet, it was no big deal. In my mind, that kind of mind-set is akin to locking car doors only when it holds something of value. If you think for a moment, you should realize that aside from the passengers, the car itself is likely more valuable than anything inside it. An unlocked vehicle is only inviting car theft. Even pre-owned cars today can cost well in excess of $10,000, on average. Doesn't it make sense to try to protect them? How many people carry $10,000 in cash with them?

I once worked as a computer repair technician traveling to a very remote area of northern Arizona. This particular company had placed their server in the men's bathroom. I literally had to sit on the toilet in order to work on the computer. This most certainly was not the high point of my computer career. Aside from the obvious lack of physical security, you can imagine this system was not protected very well from the elements. (I'll spare you the specifics.)

PROTECT YOUR COMPUTERS FROM THE ELEMENTS

Take care not to place servers, or even workstations or laptops, in places where they may be exposed to rain, dust, moisture, or other elements that can get them dirty and cause them to malfunction. I have seen computers placed in areas where the ventilation was so bad that the entire inside of the computer was crammed full of dust bunnies. Think about what happens to your vacuum cleaner when the bag gets too full. Just as a clogged vacuum cleaner won't operate properly, a clogged computer can fail as well. In one convenience store, a computer was placed dangerously close to the soda fountain. Soda is far too syrupy and sticky to be a good neighbor for computers.

It is also important to protect computers from extremes of either heat or cold. A computer's hard drive spins at speeds of up to 10,000 times per minute, depending on the model. That can generate a fair amount of heat. Computers can easily burn out if not given sufficient ventilation or if exposed to high enough temperatures. A frozen computer isn't much better than an overheated one. So make sure that your computers get adequate ventilation, and protect them from extremes of either heat or cold. Obviously, rain, sleet, and snow won't do a computer any good, either.

COMPUTERS AND ELECTRICITY

You can take other measures to protect your computers, whether at home or in your business. Make sure that they have a good, clean source of electrical power. Computers react badly to fluctuations in electricity. A good way to protect computers from sudden unexpected spikes in power is to use a surge suppressor. Many surge suppressors can also act as a power strip and accommodate six or more electrical devices. They are relatively inexpensive, and you can get them at electronics stores, computer stores, and even stores like Target and Wal-Mart. I recommend surge suppressors not only for your computers, but also for your televisions, stereo components, or any other piece of electronics you want protected from an expected surge of electrical power. They are a small investment that offers your computers and other expensive electronic equipment a good degree of protection. Also bear in mind that a spike in electrical power can damage a computer's hard drive, which could potentially result in data loss.

Computers react very badly to a sudden loss of electricity such as a power outage—what is commonly referred to as a blackout. While laptops have internal batteries, servers and workstations do not. You can purchase external batteries specifically designed for computers that are called Uninterrupted Power Supplies, or UPS devices. Smaller ones are fine for home systems, and you can use slightly larger ones for your business. UPS devices are designed to allow you the time you need to gracefully power off your computers so as to avoid losing data, and to avoid other technical problems caused by a power failure. They generally are not designed to act as an alternative power source that allows you to continue working. So if the power goes out, shut the computers down.

If your business model requires that your computers stay on even with a loss of main power, you'll have to obtain a reliable source of alternative energy. This could mean that you have a sufficient quantity of UPS devices to allow work to continue. However, a more common alternative form of electric power is a diesel-powered generator that can provide backup power until the main power is restored. Investing in large diesel generators and accounting for a sufficient amount of fuel to keep them running is not a cheap endeavor. Like many measures to protect computers, it should be a business decision predicated on your specific needs. If generators do fit into your business model, you will definitely want to invest in surge suppressors for your computers. Diesel generators are far more prone to power spikes than is a city's power grid.

Greater Access = Greater Risk

An unfortunate truth is that while providing your computers a degree of physical protection is important, the majority of hacking attempts are undertaken by people not located anywhere near them. That's because today's risk model is much different from what it was in years past. When computers first started to appear in offices and in the home, they were isolated systems.

There were no Internet or wide area networks. Computers were mainly used for word processing and for playing games such as Minesweeper and solitaire. It simply was not possible for a hacker located on the other side of the country, much less one located abroad, to gain access to a system that had no connectivity to the outside world.

I can remember when file sharing meant copying data to a floppy disk and walking it over to a coworker, who would then load the file onto their computer. The colloquial term used for that kind of file sharing was called "sneaker net." Even when the Internet first appeared on the scene, the risks to computers were still relatively small. That was because in the "old days," people used dial-up modems to gain access to the information superhighway. By today's standards, dial-up modems are painfully slow. Furthermore, back in the modem era, most computers were only connected to the Internet when users were actively online. Contrast that model with what we have today. Digital Subscriber Lines (or simply DSL) and cable modems are light years ahead of old-style dial-up modems in terms of speed. They are both also "always on." That combination of high speed and near-continual access has made the job of hackers and others who would use the Internet to cause mischief and harm much easier.

TURN IT OFF: AN EASY HACKER PROOFING TECHNIQUE

There is a saying in computer security that there is no such thing as making a system "hacker proof." The underlying assumption behind that statement is the supposition that the computer systems must always be powered on as well as connected to the Internet. That is actually true for businesses that sell their products and services online. Their Web servers are up and running around the clock, and hence are always a target for hackers. Consider the fact that companies like eBay and Amazon.com can't very well turn their computers off at night. That said, we are not all eBay and Amazon.com.

If you don't need your computer to be connected to the Internet all the time, then disconnect it. A computer that is not connected to the Internet is next to impossible to hack remotely. The same strategy will work for businesses as well. If your business computing needs do not require that you always be connected to the Internet, then don't be. With this simple approach, you will stop hackers cold. I often advise people that computer security risks can be thought of similarly to other risks in business. Consider the fact that every time a bank sells a mortgage, they are accepting some risk. The mortgagee can default, costing the bank money. The bank performs due diligence to make an informed decision about whether or not to loan the money to a particular customer. They will ask customers to provide information about both their income and expenses. The bank will also perform a credit check to see if the customer has a history of paying their bills on time. The bank will perform these checks to see if the benefits of selling the mortgage, i.e., the interest payments on the loan, outweigh the risks. The same cost-benefit analysis can be applied to risks involving computers. If the benefits, either to yourself or your business, don't outweigh the risks, reevaluate the situation.

In short, if you do not need to be connected to the Internet, then don't be. If you are not aware of the potential risks you might be accepting, then I humbly submit that you are reading the right book. Since the best decisions are always well-informed ones, read on.

There is an even more powerful technique that will thwart data thieves and hackers than disconnecting your computers from the Internet. For both home users and businesses alike, perhaps the most effective anti-hacker tool is to simply turn off your computers before you either leave work for the day or go to sleep at night. During the day, if the kids are at school and you are at work, don't leave your home computers on and connected to the Internet. When you shut your doors at the end of the business day, if you don't need your computers to be on, then turn them off. Not only are you saving your computers from the dangers of hacking, but you are also saving money. Whatever else computers are, they are also electronic devices. Just as you would turn off the television or the radio when not using them, consider turning off your computer as well.

I can almost hear the protests of many of my readers now. They will say, "I need to leave my computer on, at least during the day because it takes too long for it to power up, and that is just inconvenient." Not to worry; there are techniques that you can use to stop hackers that don't include powering off your computer. Hackers need your computers to be powered on *and* connected to the Internet in order to try to perform their mischief. If you were to power off either your cable modem or your DSL connection, that would take your computer off-line, and again stop hackers cold. Both cable modems and DSL connections generally power on much more quickly than computers do, so it would be less of an inconvenience to wait for them to be ready to use again. So, if you are either not using your computer at the moment, or using it but don't necessarily need the Internet, go ahead and go off-line.

There are also ways to take your computer off-line, disconnected from the Internet, without powering anything off. While they are discussed in more detail in Chapter 7, most brands of personal firewalls have a simple on/off setting that is designed to stop all Internet traffic. While they are not as fool-proof as powering off your computer or cable modem, bear in mind that the overwhelming majority of Internet hackers are not targeting you specifically.

They are looking for the unprotected computer that is online. Consider the analogy of taking the keys out of the ignition and locking your car doors. Those actions do not make it impossible for a thief to steal your vehicle. However, in a crowded parking lot, the thief most likely is not specifically looking to steal *your* car. In most cases they are just looking to steal *a* car. The car whose doors are unlocked and whose keys are sitting on the front seat is the easier target. The thief doesn't have to break in and try to hot-wire anything—it's all right there. So, while theoretically a hacker may be able to gain access to a computer whose Internet protection is the "stop all Internet connectivity" toggle switch on your personal firewall, it does make his job much more difficult.

DON'T EXPOSE YOUR SYSTEM TO HACKERS

Computers and the Internet are so wondrous—or perhaps, the term "mysterious" would be more accurate—that at times, as end-users, we cause ourselves problems. Consider a Web site such as LimeWire.com. Now, the name in and of itself isn't very descriptive. LimeWire is a Web site that allows users to install file-sharing software on their computers. This allows you to share files with people who also have LimeWire's file-sharing application on their computers. The problem with file-sharing applications such as this is that if they are not properly configured, you can inadvertently open up all of the files on your computer to others with the same application installed on their system. Don't think for a moment that hackers are not scanning computers that are online with incorrectly configured file-sharing programs on them, enabling them to easily steal whatever files off your computer that they would like. Even if properly configured, the application itself could have security flaws in it, enabling hackers to steal your data no matter what settings you use. A rule that we have in the Alexander household is that my sons are not allowed to download anything without my expressed permission. If you think I'm being too harsh, consider the implications beyond exposing the data on my computer to hackers. The software could not be compatible with your system for some reason, thus causing your computer to stop working properly.

A number of years ago, in a moment of weakness, I let my then five-year-old son install some free software that he received after getting a haircut. Family hair-care chains are not generally known for their robust software development standards. Upon loading the CD onto the family computer, the system almost immediately began having problems. Some other applications were greatly slowed down, while others didn't work at all. Fortunately, since I am a computer engineer, I was able to repair the damage caused by my momentary lapse in judgment. Just like if you let your young child borrow the family car, the resulting situation may require a qualified repairman to set things right again.

Getting qualified technical support for your computers, in and of itself, carries with it challenges beyond the obvious issues of inconvenience and cost. Depending on what type of technical support is used, that alone can introduce data security risks to your computer. It's important to be armed with information so the issue of seeking out help to resolve a computer problem isn't compounded by the actions of unscrupulous computer support technicians, causing you additional headaches.

Chapter 2

SOLVE PROBLEMS WHILE NEUTRALIZING NOSY TECH SUPPORT

It is a fact of life that most of us need to call for technical support for our computers every now and then. In the spirit of full disclosure, even a veteran such as myself, with over 20 years of computer experience, has had to call technical support from time to time for assistance in resolving a computer issue. It is not at all uncommon for companies to offer many different types of support, including online support, for the computers, printers, applications, etc., that they sell. In the "good old days," technical support was limited to either user manuals or working through the problem with a help desk technician over the telephone. Today, with the advent of the Internet in conjunction with high-speed connectivity, technical support is available in a myriad of ways. While this has most certainly made resolving computer problems easier in many instances, it has also had some unintended consequences.

SUPPORT BY REMOTE CONTROL

It happens to all of us. We buy the new computer, and along with it, a new printer that is not just a printer, but can also copy, fax, scan—just about everything but brew coffee. And then there are the innumerable gadgets that we can connect to our computers to further enhance, and sometimes complicate, our technological experience. A recent trend that I have seen is for companies that provide technical support to request to be able to take information right off of their customers' computers.

For example, if you were to go to Hewlett-Packard's Web site and try to work with online technical support, and you see the following:

HP Chat has the ability to display system information to our online technicians to help them better diagnose and resolve your product issue. HP upholds strict customer privacy guidelines, and our online technicians will not access your personal files. Please click below to allow HP to collect this system information.[1]

Then it asks you to choose "I accept" or "I do not accept."

I had a similar experience when I contacted Dell Computers seeking help with troubleshooting a problem that I was having with the e-mail program native to Microsoft Vista Home Edition. In that case, the technical support person on the other end of the phone told me that I needed to allow him to take remote control of my computer. The purpose, so he claimed, was so he could investigate the problem and fix it for me.

Aside from many of the large computer hardware and software vendors, a whole slew of companies provide online remote technical support for home and smallbusiness computer systems. Like Dell or HP, many of them ask you to grant their service technicians remote control of your computer system in order to help them diagnose technical problems. Here are a few examples taken directly from the Web sites of some such companies.

This is what a user will find when they visit the Web site of a typical company seeking assistance with a computer problem.

> **Remote PC Doctor** is the core of our company's diagnostic software suite, Tecky-Connect. By using it, our technicians are able to remotely diagnose and repair of your PC. You can download Remote PC Doctor from our website and install onto your computer. TeckyConnect will make our further service quicker, easier and more effective. Once installed on your computer TeckyConnect will appear in your Start menu as well as in Program files. This will enable you to more easily access our services. The program will also install an icon on the Desktop of your computer allowing you to get there by a simple click of the mouse.
>
> **TeckyConnect** Our special diagnostic software saves you time. It takes just a few minutes for it to determine what software is installed on your PC. This will eliminate the need for you to answer technical questions about your computer to which you might not have the answers.
>
> **Perform accurate diagnoses.** The TeckyConnect software will scan your PC for conflicts, errors and malfunctions, thus enabling our Experts to resolve problems much faster,
>
> **Get immediate response.** Our proprietary software performs all diagnostics and repairs in real-time.. This allows us to start processing your inquiries immediately. The installation and use of TeckyConnect does not require special computer knowledge. All you have to do is to follow the simple instructions on the screen. The diagnostic data will be collected and sent back to our Experts automatically.
>
> **The** TeckyConnect **application suite includes the following components:**
>
> • **Remote PC Doctor**—collects the information about how your computer is configuration and the software that is installed on it. This data can be immediately sent to our Experts for analysis.

- **Screen Sharing**—this allows our people to control your computer over the Internet. Our Experts can more easily resolve your computer problems. They can also use it to provide you with training as well.

Most companies that provide remote computer support have privacy policies. In many cases, they'll post their privacy policy online. With some variation, a company providing remote computer support will go something like this:

> The TeckyRemoteManagement tool allows you to give control of your computer to experts remotely via the Internet, thus enabling them to diagnose or correct problems. Our experts are not allowed to use the TeckyRemote-Management software until you have consented to its use. Furthermore, our experts will not use TeckyRemoteManagement tools in order to obtain confidential or sensitive information stored on your computer or network, nor will they destroy information on your computer or network, or cause system problems.

The reason that these companies want you to grant their technical support engineers remote access to your computer is simple. It can be very challenging, hence requiring a high level of expertise, to resolve a computer problem strictly by having the customer describe what they are seeing and experiencing over the telephone. It is much easier to take control and to be able to see things for yourself. Moreover, companies can save money by hiring lesser-skilled technical support engineers who can simply take control of a customers' computer remotely to resolve the problem. The "old-fashioned way" is more difficult. Think of it in comparison to the cash registers in fast food restaurants of years past. Back in the 1970s and 1980s, you needed to know what the price of each item was and how to count back the correct change. Today's cash registers have pictures of the items for sale on them, and they tell the cashier how much change is due back to the customer. Today's cashiers don't need to have the level of mathematical knowledge their predecessors a generation before them did. Giving fast food workers cash registers that make their jobs easier doesn't change your experience in ordering a hamburger and french fries. However, allowing a technical support engineer remote access to your computer can.

In all my years working in the computer industry, I have never once heard a computer support vendor tell me that their technical support engineers were not trustworthy and that they would steal my data if given half a chance. It is also very common to have privacy statements similar to the example above touted by computer-support companies to assure clients about the safety of their data, and that there is nothing to worry about.

The hard truth is that while most technical support engineers are in fact honest, hardworking people who would not steal your data, some of them will, if given the opportunity. If I was in that dishonest "hacker minority" and I wanted to be granted access to computers so I could easily steal data, it would be very convenient to get a job working for a company providing Internet-based technical support. I would be given access to computer systems as part of my job, which would mean that I would not have to try to hack into anything. A customer would not know who I am or even where I'm located. I could very well be located in a foreign country halfway around the world. Bear in mind that offshore outsourcing, especially computer technical support, is all the rage these days. This is because the salaries of some overseas engineers can be significantly less than those of their domestic counterparts here in the United States.

Think for a moment about what the technical support engineers are asking you to do in this type of situation and what the repercussions could be. A person that you have never met is asking that you grant him or her remote access to your computer. Remember to factor into this scenario that many of us keep personal information on our home computers, such as tax records, information about a home-based business, medical records, personal family photos, and so on.

Again, I do not feel that every support person is a data thief or a hacker. Quite the contrary—most are likely to be good, honest, decent, hardworking people that would not even consider doing anything inappropriate. Most plumbers, electricians, and handymen are also decent, honest people. Yet, most of us take reasonable precautions to protect the valuables that we have in our homes when we allow strangers in to perform such work. Most people would deem it somewhat risky to leave cash, jewelry, and other valuables out in plain sight with workmen in the house. Most of us also feel safer not having workers in our homes unless either an adult family member or another trusted person is there to keep an eye on things. Again, it is not making the assumption that all workers are thieves, it is just a matter of taking reasonable steps both to safeguard our valuables and to help avoid any unfortunate incidents.

To a hacker, you are just a faceless voice on the other end of a telephone. It is much harder to pinpoint a hacker who has just stolen the data off of your computer than it is to find that plumber who has just stolen something out of your house. You saw the plumber and can make a report to the police. Such reporting is much harder, if not impossible, to do with a hacker. To make matters worse, in most instances, the hacker will not actually remove the data from your computer; she will just take a copy of it. You might not even realize that your data has been stolen until long afterwards.

That's what makes it much harder to pinpoint a crime than if a worker inside your house stole a piece of jewelry.

Granting a support technician remote access to your computer carries with it risks beyond that of hacking. Working on computers can be complex. Today's computers are not only very complicated, but they also vary quite a bit from model to model. The steps that may work to fix my computer might cause your computer to have worse problems than it had in the first place. Computers vary from manufacturer to manufacturer. The installation of a given Windows operating system varies, for instance, from a Dell to a Compaq. Each of us also loads different after-market software applications onto our computers. These not-so-subtle differences among computers means that there is no one simple fix to address problems. Grant a technical support engineer remote control of your computer, and you might find yourself with more problems than you started off with.

THE PROBLEM: LAZY ENGINEERING

Lazy engineering is a term that I have been using for many years. I use it to describe engineers who want take the easy way out when performing their jobs. Perhaps a more appropriate definition would be this: Lazy engineers take inappropriate shortcuts. For example, if an engineer's job is to manage printers on a large network, you can limit their powers to adding, deleting, and otherwise dealing with mundane printer tasks, in the name of security. The lazy engineer will insist that he needs total control over the entire network to be able to perform his job. That just isn't the case; in fact, it is just a case of lazy engineering. Giving the lazy engineer everything would allow him to be able to affect other things, such as data backups, e-mail, instant messaging, and other non-printer-related functions on the computer network. The lazy thought process goes something like this: "Give me every power that I might possibly need so I don't have to figure out what I really need."

I see a remote support engineer asking to be able to take remote control of a computer as yet another example of lazy engineering. Rather than working with you in diagnosing what is wrong, he just wants control of the computer to figure things out for himself. That is more power than he needs and, in my opinion, certainly more than you should grant him. The ability to work with a customer over the telephone to diagnose and resolve a computer issue takes time and effort, as well as a certain degree of skill. Companies developing the model of having their support engineers take remote control of their customer's computers is an attempt to shorten call times as well as to utilize less-seasoned (and, not coincidentally, cheaper) engineering labor.

YOU WANT WHAT?

Lazy engineering is not just limited to computer technicians providing remote support. In the name of laziness, I have had engineers ask me for everything amounting to the proverbial keys to the kingdom. Years ago, when I was a senior information security officer for a major financial institution, I had a support vendor tell me that to troubleshoot a problem that we were having with a database they built for us, they would need us to send them the entire database—contents and all. Think of a database as being your house with all its contents, including all your valuable belongings. Now, as you can imagine, this database contained sensitive information about many of our customers. As the "security guy" on the project, I set the expectation right away that there was no way we were going to send them our customer data so they could try to resolve a glitch in the database.

SQL, Oracle, and DB2 are three of the biggest database applications on the market today. In all my years, none of the three companies that sell these products ever asked me to send the entire database, information and all, so their techs could resolve a technical glitch. I know from experience what this vendor was asking for was not only extraordinary, but also unnecessary. In other words, lazy engineering: Give me everything I might possibly need, so I do not have to put forth the effort to figure out what I really need. I knew they had the technical expertise to support the database that we had purchased from them; I told them that they would have to rely on system logs and other diagnostic tools. The point: It is okay to question what you are being asked to give support engineers so they can resolve an issue for you.

If your company's or family's sensitive data is involved, proceed with caution. There is also a balance between getting your system back up and running as soon as possible and the possibility of exposing your sensitive data to a vendor's support engineer. You will need to find a balance that you are comfortable with. If you are purchasing either hardware or software, I would recommend that you have these types of discussions up front. Before money is spent, set the expectation of what kind of technical support you expect, and get it in writing. This can include response times, what forms of technical support will take place (phone, in-person, over the Internet, technical how-to manuals) and what type of data you will and will not send them. There are also companies that will sell you support contracts. Like insurance, you pay a premium that guarantees you a level of service when you have a technical problem. There again, be very up front about what type of service you expect and to what degree you will allow the support engineers to have access.

TRUST ME AND DO EXACTLY WHAT I SAY

There is a danger that goes beyond the telephone support technician being a hacker. You can very quickly find yourself in uncomfortable territory even with a computer support person who is honest. The danger is when they are asking you to perform actions on your computer that you have no knowledge of or what the consequences of such actions might be. The quandary is that in order for the computer support technician on the other end of the telephone to help you, they are going to have to ask you to perform certain actions on your computer. Depending on your personal level of technical computer knowledge, you may or may not know anything about what they are having you do. Some actions are relatively benign and can't do much harm, while others can cause serious problems. The issue then is trying to know which are which. My advice is to go slowly, double check with the computer technician before hitting keys when you're not sure what might happen next. Ask them what they are hoping to accomplish by having you perform such actions. Tell them to go at a pace that you are comfortable with. Actions that are routine to them can be a mystery to you.

Remember, you are the one with the vested interest. The remote support technician's computer is working just fine; yours is the one that is not. It is also your computer that may be further harmed by some of the actions the remote support engineer is asking you to take. I don't mean to say that they are being malicious. It is just that each computer is slightly different. The software that we load on our computers, the variations from manufacturer to manufacturer and even within the same manufacturer—all of these factors make our computers unique to a certain point. Just like as a group, we are all human beings; but individually, we are unique. General "routines" that might work fine for most people could seriously harm a specific person. For example, I am allergic to penicillin. What is a wonder drug for many could very well mean death to me. Along the same lines, a support routine that might work fine for some computers might harm yours.

TECHNICAL SUPPORT IN THE FORM OF HOUSE CALLS

Some companies, such as the Geek Squad, will send a computer repair technician to your house or place of business to help you resolve your computer issues. It is like when doctors used to make house calls in what is now a bygone era. Again, most of these people are decent, hardworking individuals. With that said, I recommend watching what they do. If they are plugging a thumb drive into your computer, ask them why they need to do that. Certainly get suspicious if they are trying to e-mail information from your computer to a Web mail account such as Yahoo or Hotmail. Even a certain amount of attentiveness is helpful. If they have mischief in mind, they are less likely to engage in nefarious activities if you are right there watching them. You also might learn something, and be able to better support your computer in the future, if you pay attention to what they are doing.

I have found that most such computer support engineers are more than happy to show you what they are doing on your computer. Back when I performed in-house PC support, I would always tell the customer what I was doing and why. I would also show them things that they could do themselves to help keep their computers working at top efficiency. It is akin to an auto mechanic telling people to maintain proper air pressure in their tires in order to get better gas mileage and to extend the life of the tires themselves.

SIMPLE COMPUTER MAINTENANCE ROUTINES

All modern versions of the Microsoft Windows operating system come with a handful of maintenance routines that can help improve computer performance. They include disk cleanup, defragmentation, and error-checking. Find the "My Computer" icon on your computer's desktop. Right click on it, and then choose "Explore." From there, right click on the computer's "C" drive and choose "Properties." The disk cleanup routine is located on the "General" tab. This will allow the system to remove unnecessary files on your computer. It can help your computer run faster and free up hard drive space as well. The error-checking and defragmentation routines are both located on the "Tools" tab. I recommend that you run the error-checking routine first, followed by the defragmentation tool. Error-checking, as the name suggests, entails both checks and attempts to repair minor errors. The defragmentation tool is basically another type of cleanup routine that is also designed to improve a computer's performance.

ONLINE AND OFF-LINE MANUALS

Many software companies will place information online on how to fix common problems that their customers experience. This can be in the form of a manual, or a frequently asked questions (FAQ) section. These can be very helpful to you in resolving their computer challenges. Some sites invite users to ask questions, and then have other users respond. This type of user forum is generally not moderated by the particular software company, nor is the information value-tested to ensure that it is, in fact, accurate. So, while such information can be very useful, I personally put more faith in information put out by the company that actually sold me the piece of hardware or software.

Then, of course, there is the good old-fashioned manual. Most computers, printers, and other pieces of electronics come with an instruction manual. They can be very helpful in both the initial setup and ongoing support of a piece of equipment. Likewise, most applications come with an instruction manual as well. While on the topic of physical manuals, there are a wide range of books out there to assist people with their computing experience. They are written for people of all skill levels, from the hardcore engineer to the general public. Many years ago, while working as a computer hardware engineer, I was chastised by my coworkers for having a "For Dummies" book on how to repair computers. I found the book to be a great resource, and the truth is that we all need a little help every once in a while.

Exercise Due Care with What You Share

In the name of technical troubleshooting, it's not uncommon for the application to ask you to send out the error messages that you are seeing on your computer. In some cases, such requests are automated. An example of this is when a Microsoft application, such as Internet Explorer, has a malfunction. A message will pop up on the computer screen asking if you want to send a report about the error to them. On the one hand, I can see the value in providing Microsoft with such information. It enables them to identify bugs in their programs to be able to develop fixes for them faster. With that said, I am concerned about the nature of information that is included in these error reports. Is it strictly technical data, or might it contain some of my personal data as well? Consider Microsoft's statement about the data it collects in error reports. "We do not intentionally collect your name, address, email address or any other form of personally identifiable information. However, the error report *may contain customer-specific information in the collected data files.* While this *information could potentially be used to determine your identity,* if present, it will not be used" (emphasis added). The bottom line is that Microsoft comes right out and states that their error reports may contain your personal data. So, while I'd like to help, the security of my personal data is more important to me.

The reasons for my not sending Microsoft their error reports go beyond the concern for my personal data. I am also concerned about the nature of the technical data that they collect. An unfortunate truth is that the same information that can help a software manufacturer troubleshoot their applications can also help a hacker to attack your computer more easily. The more a hacker knows about a computer, its operating system, and what kind of software it is using and the versions thereof, the better able they are to successfully attack it. The reason for this is that many software products have known vulnerabilities, so knowing what you have installed on your computer will allow the hacker to craft an attack designed specifically to exploit them. It is actually a common attack methodology for a hacker to submit requests to a Web site that are specifically designed to cause errors so that the site will return messages containing information that they can turn around and try and use to better hack the back-end systems. That is whyI never send error reports back when prompted to by the pop-up windows. A few less reports among Microsoft's millions of customers won't impact its ability to fix any glitches in its software.

The "blind" sending of error data over the Internet is different from working with a technical support person who is trying to help you resolve an issue that you're having with your computer. She will, at times, ask you to tell her what you are seeing on your computer screen as you perform certain tests. A certain amount of cooperation in a situation like that is important if you want him to be able to help you fix your computer.

DATA THEFT BY FILE TYPE

I can almost hear my critics now: I'm being an alarmist—especially with computer hard drives being so large. There's no way a remote technician can find anything worth stealing in the short time that they are connected to my computer. It is like trying to find the proverbial needle in a haystack. But consider this: If I wanted to steal all Word documents on a computer, I would seek out files that ended in *.doc*. If I was looking for Excel spreadsheets, it would be *.xls*. If you do your own taxes, and a hacker wanted to steal your financial data, they would look for files ending in *.tax*. There are other examples, of course, but the point is simple: A data thief could perform a targeted search for specific file types that the majority of us use to store our sensitive personal data. Also bear in mind that most people use very descriptive names when labeling data files. So, files with names such as "health records," "last will and testament," "financial data," or simply "$$$" are strong indications of files that contain sensitive data—that is, information that a hacker could use to commit either identity theft, financial fraud, or both. A hacker could also steal the contents of a user's "My Documents" folder, the default location where many of us store our documents.

DATA THEFT—POST CONNECTIVITY

The would-be data thief also does not have to limit himself to trying to steal data during the time he is connected directly to your computer.

He can simply install some malware on your computer. Malware is a type of program that will seek out files and then e-mail them back to the hacker at a later time. The target may not even be the data that is on your computer. The hacker may be installing malware on your computer to turn it into what's called a "zombie." Like the name suggests, a hacker can use a zombie computer to perform hacking attacks on his behalf automatically. This has a number of advantages for the hacker. A skilled hacker with the right amount of patience can turn hundreds, or even thousands, of computers into zombies. This would increase the effectiveness of the hacker's true target, with his computerized zombie army attacking at the hacker's command. It will also make finding and prosecuting the hacker difficult, if not impossible, since his computer was not actively involved in the actual attack. For example, take an attack against a government computer or of a major private-sector company. Imagine how you would feel if somebody were to contact you and ask you why your computer was trying to attack a government network.

VICARIOUS LIABILITY

There have been instances in which businesses have been held civilly liable for allowing their computers to be used by hackers to mount malicious attacks. The culpability usually lies in the fact that businesses have not maintained their computer systems to a reasonable industry standard, thus making them more easily taken over by hackers and turned into zombies. It is a recognized fact that having unprotected computers that are attached to the Internet can give hackers the added processing power needed to carry out more damaging attacks. Aside from the civil liability aspect, as a security guy, I would like to believe that people do not want their computers used by hackers to carry out attacks against either the government or other companies. If nothing else, hackers take a certain amount of computing and network capacity away from your systems in order to utilize them for their own nefarious purposes. Businesses certainly do not want to subsidize hacking and have their own network performance suffer in the process.

REGULATORY FINES

Most U.S. states have enacted data breach laws requiring that companies provide notice to affected customers in the event that their personal data has been stolen. These requirements apply not only to large companies, but to small mom-and-pop businesses as well. Examples of sensitive information covered by such regulations could include health care information that you keep on file about your employees. If your business accepts credit cards, and you keep records that contain customers' names and account numbers, that's protected data as well. Industry estimates place the cost of lost customer data at around $198 per record. At that price, the fines and penalties for a breach can be financially crippling, depending on the number of customers that are affected. You should also consider the fact that part of that per-record amount takes into account that your customers might also come after you if they fall victim to identity theft as a result of your company losing their personal data. In short, data security isn't just for banks anymore.

It has been said that the most secure computer in the world is the one that you know exactly what it is doing, does only what you want it to do, and does nothing else. I have yet to find that computer. I honestly doubt that such a computer exists. It is simply not possible to know everything that your computer, with its hundreds of programs and untold volumes of data, is doing. That's why it's important to exercise due care in not only knowing what data we store on our computers, but more importantly, where that data might be going. That can be either with or without our knowledge or implied consent.

NOTE

1. http://ipgweb.cce.hp.com/ipgna/caller/chat.asp?dd=aio&productName=HP +Officejet+6310+All-in-One&productCategory=12019&SCOID=238445 &PSOID=1120059&lang=en&cc=us.

Chapter 3

KNOW WHERE PERSONAL AND CUSTOMER DATA GOES

In today's computing age, our personal data is everywhere. I find it rather disconcerting when sales people ask me for personal information when I am either buying goods or obtaining certain services. If banks (and other such companies we trust to secure our information) are losing data, just how secure is our information that is being housed at the corner video rental store going to be? I'm lumping into this category companies that ask for personal information when making purchases online, as well as the more traditional brick-and-mortar stores. They both have some similar data security concerns as well as risks unique unto themselves.

SHOPPING ONLINE

As we are now fully into the twenty-first century, you can purchase almost anything over the Internet. The most common way of doing so will require that you provide your credit card information in order to pay for the item you want to purchase. (PayPal, an alternative to providing an individual online retailer with your credit card information, is discussed later.) The vast majority of online retail outlets encrypt the data while it is being transmitted from your computer to their site. You can easily verify this by looking for a small gold-colored padlock that is located immediately to the right of the site address. The padlock means that the Web site is using Secure Socket Layer (or simply SSL) encryption, which is the current industry standard for protecting data while it is being transmitted over the Internet. A number of companies, such as VeriSign and Equifax, issue the digital certificates that allow for the SSL encryption. A nice feature is that you can position your mouse pointer over the gold-colored padlock icon and left click on it to verify the identity of the site. The Web site's identity is verified by the information provided when you click on the padlock. Is something like this possible for a creative hacker to fake? Sure. However, there is a difference between due diligence and outright paranoia. We need to have a certain level of trust if we want to use the Internet.

Many Web sites will ask you if you want the system to remember your credit card information so you will not have to enter it again for subsequent purchases. I have mixed feelings about this. On one hand, the ever-cautious part of my nature leads me to say no. Just use my credit card for the one transaction, and that is it. On the other hand, once you have made a purchase with your credit card, they have the information. How they protect it is, of course, unknown. It would also be wrong to assume that once they have completed the one transaction that they would not keep your credit card information on file anyway. Bearing that in mind, does it really add any additional risk for the convenience of not having to reenter your credit card information for subsequent purchases? In most cases, what you will see displayed on your screen in subsequent purchases is the credit card type (MasterCard, Visa, Discover, American Express, etc.) and the last four digits of the card number.

Companies that accept credit card payments are also very heavily regu-lated. A number of the major credit card issuers, including Visa, MasterCard, Discover, and American Express, collaborated to develop a standard for the protection of consumers' credit card information. The Payment Card Indus-try, or PCI, has established strict guidelines on the use and protection of credit card account information. Just how vigorously they are policing all the companies out there is another thing.

If you are concerned about making purchases online using a credit card, you can do a number of things to help protect yourself. Consider having a credit card dedicated for making online purchases. It means that you will get a monthly statement dedicated solely to your online purchases, making it easier to detect any fraudulent activity. Of course, it is equally important to check all credit card statements regularly. Such a dedicated credit card serves as a data-filtering mechanism. In addition to being able to more easily identify and stop unauthorized online purchases made with your "dedicated" credit card, you will also be able to more easily spot any fraudulent online purchases made with your other cards. If you are going to have a dedicated credit card for making online purchases, consider keeping the credit limit low. This too will help avoid fraudsters who are looking for the "big score."

Prepaid credit cards are another way to limit your liability. If your avail-able line of credit is only a couple of hundred dollars, the fraudster can't rack up thousands of dollars in illegal charges.

If you do suspect that any fraudulent purchases have been made with your credit card, or see other billing errors on your statement, call the issuer right away. All credit card companies place a toll-free 800 number on the back of their cards. You can call in to report suspected fraud any time day or night.

YOUR LEGAL RIGHTS REGARDING DISPUTED CREDIT CARD CHARGES

In the event that somebody does use your credit card to make fraudulent purchases, your liability is limited to $50. You won't be stuck having to pay for the hundreds or even thousands of dollars of illegal purchases that a fraudster has made with your credit card. Some credit card issuers have even lowered the liability from $50 down to $0. The $50 limit in liability is actually set by law under the Fair Credit Billing Act (FCBA). You may dispute billing errors on your credit card under the following areas:

- Your liability for unauthorized charges on your credit card is limited to $50, per the FCBA.
- Charges that list the wrong date or amount.
- Charges for goods and services you didn't order, don't accept, or weren't delivered as agreed.
- Math errors.
- You are not liable for your creditor's failure to post payments and other credits, such as returns to your account.
- If you credit card issuer failed to send bills to your current address, you may dispute errors. Late fees are common if you didn't receive your monthly statement because it was sent to the wrong address. The bill wouldn't be paid, and late fees would likely be assessed. Now, the FCBA does state that it is our responsibility to advise credit card companies of any change of address. Notify them in writing. The U.S. Postal Service allows us to have our mail forwarded to a new address for up to 12 months; that should provide plenty of time to notify creditors and anybody else of a change of address.
- Those charges for which you ask for an explanation or written proof of purchase along with a claimed error or request for clarification.

As consumers, we have to take action to protect ourselves from charges that we feel are incorrect. The FCBA states that in order to take advantage of the law's consumer protections, you must:

- Write to the creditor at the address given for "billing inquiries," not the address for sending your payments. This is important since in most cases, the addresses are, in fact, different. When writing to make a billing inquiry, the law requires that you include your name, address, account number, and a description of the billing error.
- The FCBA also states that you need to send your letter so that it reaches the creditor within 60 days after the first bill containing the error was mailed to you. So if you have a dispute, don't delay.

If you're unable to resolve the issue with your creditor over the phone, send the letter to the creditor immediately. Also, keep records of the dates and times when you called your creditor. That information may prove very useful if the dispute turns out to be difficult to resolve.

It's a good idea that you send your letter by certified mail, return receipt requested, so you have proof of what the creditor received. Be sure that you send copies (not originals) of sales slips or other documents that support your position. Keep a copy of your dispute letter for your records until the issue is fully resolved.

Under the FCBA, the creditor must acknowledge your complaint in writing within 30 days after receiving it, unless the problem has been resolved. The FCBA also requires that the creditor must resolve the dispute within two billing cycles (but not more than 90 days) after receiving your letter.

The Federal Trade Commission's (FTC) Web site even provides a sample letter to help assist people in what a letter to their credit card company should look like:

Date
Your Name
Your Address
Your City, State, Zip Code
Your Account Number

Name of Creditor
Billing Inquiries
Address
City, State, Zip Code

Dear Sir or Madam:
I am writing to dispute a billing error in the amount of $_____ on my account. The amount is inaccurate because [describe the problem]. I am requesting that the error be corrected, that any finance and other charges related to the disputed amount be credited as well, and that I receive an accurate statement.
Enclosed are copies of [use this sentence to describe any enclosed information, such as sales slips, payment records] supporting my position. Please investigate this matter and correct the billing error as soon as possible.

Sincerely,
Your name
Enclosures: [List what you are enclosing.]

WHAT HAPPENS WHILE MY BILL IS IN DISPUTE?

According to the FTC,[1] legally, you can choose to withhold payment on the disputed amount (and related charges) while the investigation is going on. However, that is just for any charges, fees, and penalties involved in the dispute itself. You still need to pay any part of the bill not in question, including finance charges on the undisputed amount.

The FCBA also states that a creditor may not take any legal or other action to collect the disputed amount and related charges (including finance charges) during the investigation. While your account cannot be closed or restricted, the disputed amount may be applied against your credit limit.

WILL MY CREDIT RATING BE AFFECTED?

Beyond the issue of not wanting to have to pay for charges that we feel are invalid, the other issue that people often wonder about is whether or not this will negatively affect their credit ratings. The law states that a creditor may not threaten your credit rating or report you as delinquent while your bill is in dispute. However, the creditor may report that you are challenging your bill. In addition, the Equal Credit Opportunity Act prohibits creditors from discriminating against credit applicants who exercise their rights, in good faith, under the FCBA. Simply put, you cannot be denied credit simply because you've disputed a bill.

WHAT IF...

The Bill Is Incorrect?

If your bill did in fact contain an error, the law requires that you creditor must explain to you—in writing—the corrections that will be made to your account. In addition to crediting your account, the creditor must remove all finance charges, late fees, or other charges related to the error.

If the creditor determines that you owe a portion of the disputed amount, it is required to provide you with a written explanation. You are entitled by law to request that it provide you with copies of documents proving you owe the money.

The Bill Is Correct?

If the creditor's investigation determines the bill is correct, you must be told promptly and in writing how much you owe and why. You have the legal right to ask for copies of relevant documents. At this point, you'll owe the disputed amount plus any finance charges that accumulated while the amount was in dispute. You also may have to pay the minimum amount you missed paying because of the dispute.

If you still disagree with the results of the investigation, the laws state that you may write to the creditor, and you may indicate that you refuse to pay the disputed amount. However, the law states that you must act within 10 days after receiving the explanation from your creditor. At this point, the creditor may begin collection procedures against you. But if the creditor reports you to a credit bureau as delinquent, the report also must state that you don't think you owe the money. The law also requires that your creditor must tell you who gets these reports.

The Creditor Fails to Follow the Procedure?

If the disputed charges were in fact accurate, but the creditor fails to follow the procedures as outlined in the FCBA, they lose much of their ability to recover monies owed to them. The laws states that any creditor who fails to follow the settlement procedure may not collect the amount in dispute, or any related finance charges up to $50, even if the bill turns out to be correct. For example, if a creditor acknowledges your complaint in 45 days—15 days too late—or takes more than two billing cycles to resolve a dispute, the penalty applies. The penalty also applies if a creditor threatens to report, or improperly reports, your failure to pay to anyone during the dispute period.

It is important to note that disputes about the quality of goods and services are not "billing errors," so the dispute procedure does not apply. However, if you buy unsatisfactory goods or services with a credit or charge card, you can take the same legal actions against the card issuer as you can take under state law against the seller.

To take advantage of this protection regarding the quality of goods or services, you must:

- Have made the purchase (it must be for more than $50) in your home state or within 100 miles of your current billing address.
- Have made a good-faith effort to resolve the dispute with the seller first.

The dollar and distance limitations don't apply if the seller also is the card issuer, or if a special business relationship exists between the seller and the card issuer.

OTHER BILLING RIGHTS

Businesses that offer "open end" credit also must:

- Give you a written notice when you open a new account—and at certain other times—that describes your right to dispute billing errors.
- Provide a statement for each billing period in which you owe—or they owe you—more than one dollar.
- Send your bill at least 14 days before the payment is due—if you have a period within which to pay the bill without incurring additional charges.
- Credit all payments to your account on the date they are received, unless no extra charges would result if they failed to do so. Creditors are permitted to set some reasonable rules for making payments—for example, setting a reasonable deadline for payment to be received to be credited on the same date.
- Promptly credit or refund overpayments and other amounts owed to your account. This applies to instances in which your account is owed more than one dollar. Your account must be credited promptly with the amount owed. If you prefer a refund, they are required to mail it to you within seven business days after the creditor receives your written request. The creditor must also make a good-faith effort to refund a credit balance that has remained on your account for more than six months.

SUING THE CREDITOR

You can sue a creditor who violates the FCBA. If you win, you may be awarded damages, plus twice the amount of any finance charge—as long as it's between $100 and $1,000. The court also may order the creditor to pay your attorney's fees and costs. A word of caution here: The word "may" is not the same as the word "shall." There's no guarantee that the court will order the creditor to pay your attorney's fees and costs.

With that caveat in mind, if possible, hire a lawyer who is willing to accept the amount awarded to you by the court as the entire fee for representing you. Some lawyers may not take your case unless you agree to pay their fee—win or lose—or add it to the court-awarded amount if they think it's too low.

REPORTING FCBA VIOLATIONS

To file a complaint or to get free information on consumer issues, you can go to http://www.ftc.gov or call, tollfree, 1-877-FTC-HELP (1-877-382-4357);

TTY: 1-866-653-4261. The FTC enters Internet, telemarketing, identity theft, and other fraud-related complaints into Consumer Sentinel, which is a secure online database available to hundreds of civil and criminal law enforcement agencies in the United States and abroad.

As you can see, under the law it is incumbent upon you as the credit card holder to report fraudulent use when you suspect something is wrong. That is why it is so important to be vigilant and do things such as thoroughly reviewing your monthly credit card statements. Most credit card companies will also contact you if they detect purchases that are not consistent with your normal purchasing practices. For instance, if your credit card purchases average a total of $500 per month, and then a $1,000 purchase is made on a single transaction, that incident may result in your credit card company calling you to verify that this uncharacteristic purchase was legitimate. They may also opt to place a hold on your credit card. That means that you won't be able to use it until you call them and explain the purchase that they identified as unusual. This has happened to me, and the people at the credit card company are always very helpful, often apologizing for the inconvenience of either calling me, or placing a hold on my credit card. In my view, I appreciate that the company is looking out for me and helping to protect me from fraud. Do they make mistakes when credit card charges are, in fact, legitimate? The obvious answer is that of course, they do; no system is perfect. However, I'd much rather deal with the inconvenience of calling my credit card company if that call helps to keep me from becoming a crime statistic.

I don't want to leave the topic of working with your credit card company to resolve these types of issues without talking about the potential for scams. Your credit card company will never send you an e-mail advising you that there is a problem with your card and then directing you go to a Web site and require that you enter in your account information. E-mails like that constitute a specific type of scam known as phishing, which is discussed in greater detail in Chapter 7. They are, in short, a hacker's attempt to trick you into providing them with your credit card information so they can make illegal purchases.

Similar due diligence is advisable when you receive a phone call to discuss an issue with your card. If you have any doubt that the call is actually from your credit card issuer, simply hang up and call your credit card company back using the toll-free number that is on the back of the card. Another fraudster trick is to call people claiming to be from the credit card company in hopes that you will give them your account number and expiration date. They can get your name and phone number from a number of online services that provide such information, or even a good old-fashioned phone book. The fraudster has already obtained that information in order to call you in the first place.

PAYPAL

A way to make online purchases without giving companies your credit card information is to use PayPal. The online companies from whom you are buying, as well as Internet fraudsters for that matter, will only see your PayPal account, and not your credit card account information. You can deposit money into your PayPal account on an as-needed basis, as well. There is no minimum dollar amount that you need to keep on hand with PayPal. This means that even if you have reservations about PayPal itself, you can limit the amount of money in your account, thus limiting your potential losses. The majority of PayPal's services are free to use, and they do not charge an annual fee. Even receiving payments is free for personal accounts. PayPal does charge a fee for businesses to receive payments. They also charge a fee for performing currency exchanges such as changing U.S. dollars to Euros. A complete list of their services and fees can be found at http://www.PayPal.com.

I mention PayPal not only because of the services that it provides, but also to demonstrate that in many cases, there are ways to meet the needs of business while at the same time limiting your security exposure. I am often discouraged when I hear people claim how security is inconvenient and is always an impediment to business, as well as to both computer and network performance. That simply is not the case, as the PayPal example demonstrates. I have often asked people just how well their computer network would perform if it was infested with computer viruses and continually under assault by hackers. Properly implemented, security can enhance performance and be an asset to the business. I would also ask people to consider which is more of an inconvenience—taking reasonable measures to keep your credit cards secure, or dealing with your credit cards being used by fraudsters and hackers. Certainly anybody that has ever been the victim of identity theft knows what a mess that can be to try to straighten out.

BRICK-AND-MORTAR

While making credit card purchases online has its own unique risks, paying for items in more traditional brick-and-mortar stores is not without risks either. It is important to keep in mind that just like with online purchases, when making credit card purchases, you will be giving the brick-and-mortar store all the information it needs to complete the transaction. The unknown is how well it protects your credit card information as well as how long they keep that information on file. There is no level of consistency here, so do not be surprised if the company you purchased clothes from five years ago still has all of your credit card information in their computers or even printed on a piece of paper and locked away in a filing cabinet.

Perhaps one of the biggest leaps of faith that we all take is when we hand our credit card over to a waiter or waitress to pay for the meal that we have just completed. They disappear, often for five minutes or more, to run our credit card and bring us back a receipt (hoping for a generous tip, of course). Consider that in most cases, we are handing our credit cards over to complete strangers, trusting that they will use them only for the intended purpose. Yes, most waiters and waitresses are very honest people, and would never consider defrauding their customers. However, for the small percentage that are not honest, taking down our credit card information would be very simple. Again, we freely give them our credit cards and think nothing of it as they disappear from sight. They could write down all the information they would need to be able to fraudulently use the card later.

But wait, it gets worse. Why even bother writing everything down, when you can use a "wedge"? A wedge is a device that can read the data off the magnetic strip of a credit or debit card just by swiping it, similar to a legitimate card reader. Unlike a "real" card reader that sends the data to the issuer in order to obtain approval for the purchase, a wedge stores the data locally on the device. At their own convenience, the fraudsters can then connect the wedge to their computer and download all the stolen information. This practice almost makes me want to pay for everything with cash; but, of course, then I would have to worry about pickpockets and muggers. Also, as with all the risks specific to both credit and debit cards, if they are lost or stolen, you can call the issuer and cancel them. It is difficult to do that with lost or stolen cash.

THEY ARE SENDING MY DATA WHERE?

What can be even scarier is finding out exactly where companies are sending your data—sometimes ignorance really is bliss. Will they post your data in a shared database where it can be accessed by other companies? When you try to sell your house, for example, you will magically get mail from any number of local moving companies trying to sell you their services. They are obviously performing data mining of newly listed houses and trying to drum up business. This type of data sharing is one thing, but another practice that I find more disturbing it that many companies will sell your data outright to others. There are companies that will pay good money for access to customer information. How many of us ask for the data privacy statement of a company before we make a purchase using our credit or debit cards? The hard and plain truth is that none of us do. Even I am not that diligent, or perhaps, paranoid would be a better term. Another truth is that the sales clerk waiting on you at the local department store is not going to have any idea what their company's data privacy policies are. In their defense, probably half the executives in the company don't have any idea, either. The senior buyer for a major clothing store is not going to be well versed in the company's policies on protecting the privacy of the credit card information collected on their customers.

WHAT ABOUT HEALTH INFORMATION?

I am not convinced it would be much easier if you were asking the same question to your health care provider. On the one hand, companies that provide medical services are regulated on how they must protect your records. The Health Insurance Portability and Accountability Act (HIPAA) does, in fact, place strict rules on how patient medical records are to be protected. When you go to a doctor's office it is not uncommon for them to give you what is commonly referred to as a HIPAA privacy statement, which affirms that the office abides by the regulations. That said, how many workers in a given hospital know how your medical records are being stored and protected beyond what is printed on the HIPAA privacy statement that they hand out?

Sharing and selling personal data is one thing. What can be even scarier is when a company sends your personal data offshore as a normal part of their business practices. It is not uncommon for companies to send medical records and tax information to other countries for processing and storage. There are tax preparation companies that send the data offshore in order to be able to capitalize on the less-expensive labor. Their involvement in the preparation of your tax returns is often limited to spot checking the work performed by the worker located halfway around the world. If you do not want your personal financial data sent outside of the country by your tax preparer, discuss it with the firm up front—before handing your information over to them. Demand, in writing, a statement that your taxes will be prepared locally, and that your data will not be sent offshore.

There are similar concerns with health records, as the amount of paperwork involved to file health claims has become so burdensome that companies have begun to try to realize the dollar savings of the cheaper offshore labor. That one is a little trickier for the consumer to control. If your health care coverage is through your employer, you are not going to have a lot of say into whether or not your medical information is ever sent offshore. If you do have input into deciding which insurance company your business will choose to provide coverage for your employees, ask them if they send health records offshore. You may think that one small business can't change an industry, but you would be surprised how a single voice joined by others can quickly become a chorus.

Companies track lost business and the causes thereof. Once the dollar savings of sending information offshore is offset by lost business, they will begin to reconsider their position. A number of state governments are also considering legislation that will put limits on what type of information companies can send outside of the United States.

A number of high-profile data breaches over the years have got the attention of our elected officials, and they have begun to pass a slew of laws requiring businesses to protect the data of their residents. These laws often include financial penalties on a per-record basis if data is breached. If a single breach includes a large number of records, it can get very expensive very quickly. This is yet another issue for companies to factor in when deciding what data to send offshore. All of a sudden, that cheap foreign labor is getting more expensive.

I am often met with a certain amount of skepticism when I discuss the concerns of sending personal data offshore. I'm asked if I don't think people living outside of the United States are as honest and trustworthy as we Americans are. While that may be an interesting philosophical question, it's not the crux of my argument. I will happily concede the point that there are honest, hardworking people in all corners of the globe. I will also point out that there are also dishonest people living in every country around the world, including here in the United States. So the question then is, why should we trust an American with our data any more than people living in China, India, Pakistan, Russia, and so on? On a purely objective basis, I can list a number of reasons.

For one thing, many of the countries that I have listed above don't have vigorous data privacy laws like those here in the United States. As an American, if I am caught using my position as an employee of a bank or a hospital to commit data fraud, my career is done. In addition to getting fired, the odds of my ever getting a job that is considered in a position of trust are next to nil. If my crime is severe enough, in addition to my newly found career challenges, I could face state and federal charges and face years behind bars. Even if the countries do have data privacy laws, in most cases they are not as rigorously enforced as they are here in America.

A hard truth is that many of the countries that we outsource to have an active spy network. Fair is fair; we spy on other countries also. The point is, are we really sure that the data entry clerk located in a offshore branch isn't actually an employee of the foreign government engaged in data-gathering activities (spying) against the United States? It goes without saying that if the data entry clerk were to commit an act that we would consider an inappropriate use or breach of our personal data, when that person is actually an employee of the government, the said employee/spy isn't going to face any charges of any kind.

Another limitation of many foreign governments is in background checks. In most instances, the checks are regional. It's much easier to move from town to town and have a "clean" background check. So, even if you were to get fired for misusing data in a company in one town, the odds are you could still get a similar job in a different region.

Another almost insurmountable issue is that of extradition and prosecution. Even if you have a foreign hacker dead to rights, consider the level of effort it would take to have them extradited from across the ocean back to the United States. Many large companies are not willing to take on that kind of expense, much less smaller companies. That assumes, of course, that the government in question would even allow for such an extradition in the first place.

CRIMINALS: "I CARE MORE ABOUT MY COUNTRY THAN I DO ABOUT YOURS"

Now let's move from the objective to the openly opinionated. A number of years ago, I attended a summit in Washington, DC, on offshore outsourcing. One of the topics was the fact that many of us here are U.S.-centric. This can be attributed to a sense of patriotism and national pride. Well, citizens of around the world in many cases are just as proud of their country as we are of ours. My purely opinionated argument then is that as an American, even if I were of questionable ethics, I would care less about committing a data breach and risking serious harm to a company located in a foreign country than I would about one located in the United States. This is especially true if I particularly didn't care for that specific country. A case in point is that, at the conference, representatives of the Indian government were asked how they would feel about outsourcing work to neighboring Pakistan. The dead silence spoke volumes.

STORING HEALTH INFORMATION ONLINE

A relatively new phenomenon is companies offering a service that allows people to store their health records online. I personally find this incredible, especially when you consider that the single greatest source of hacking attacks and data breaches is the Internet. This is where we're supposed to store our health records—the Internet? In all fairness, some of the companies that are doing this are large, well-established organizations. That said, knowing how to maintain an Internet presence is one thing, but knowing how to properly safeguard sensitive information such as people's health records is totally different. I would never use any company's online service to store my personal health information. If the company's computers were hacked, you could very quickly find your personal health records being flashed all over the World Wide Web. Many companies struggle with a concept called separation of duties. So another question would be, "How do I know that the engineers working for them that are maintaining their computers don't have access to my medical records?" Like most entities that deal with personal information, companies that are looking to store your health records online will have a written privacy statement. Most will say that they won't sell, rent, or share your information with other companies without your consent.

Be careful here; we live in the day and age of mega-organizations that are made up of many divisions. Your health records may very well be shared internally within different divisions of the same company that is storing your health records for you. It's akin to opening a checking account at a bank, and all of a sudden, you're getting solicitations for a whole slew of other financial products the bank offers.

Most of the privacy statements also allow companies to share your health records under certain circumstances, including such things as government requests, or investigations when a company thinks you've violated the terms of its service or engaged in fraud, or when the company thinks it or its customers are at risk for any reason.

HEALTH RECORDS OF THE RICH AND FAMOUS

If you're a person of any amount of fame, whether it is as an actor, a professional athlete, a captain of industry, or a politician, I strongly suggest that you not store your health records online. The pressures to access your health records would be enormous. How much would one side pay to know that their political opponent was taking antidepressant medication? How quickly would it spread across the Internet that a young child actor was being treated for a sexually transmitted disease? Obviously, there are many more such scenarios. The point is that it's hard enough for celebrities to be able to enjoy simple private pleasures that most of us take for granted. They don't need to compound issues by placing their health records online, and hence at risk.

LOST DATA

Computers are not perfect, and they can and do fail from time to time. If you opt to store your health records online, which I advise against, at least don't let it be the only place where you have your health records. Aside from data loss due to computer problems, consider what could happen if the company that's storing your records online for you went out of business.

You could find yourself without access to your health records. What would a company do as they were going out of business? Would they contact all of their customers and make arrangements to return their health records to them? Would they exercise due care to be sure that all of the health records on their systems were properly destroyed? Would they make sure to delete your health information off of all computers before they sold them off? A more likely scenario would be that they would sell their computer assets for as much as they could, putting minimal effort and expense into ensuring the security of the data that they contain.

Such risks are not limited to the scenario of a company going out of business. A company that is taken over (purchased) now has a different set of policies and procedures. The agreements on how your data would be safe-guarded may no long be valid. Also consider what happens if you change your mind and ask for your health records back. Assuming the company sends you back your health records, what assurances do you have that they have deleted all instances of your information from their system? The truth is that you don't, and that your health records will likely be on computer hard drives and backup tapes for years to come.

As you can see, as computer users, we are faced with a number of chal-lenges in not only keeping our systems safe, but also keeping the data that we store on them safe. There are times when we must make decisions between convenience and security. That is certainly true in the area of remote access, as you will find out in the next chapter.

NOTE

1. Some of the following material on credit card issues is adapted from Federal Trade Commission information. For more, see http://www.ftc.gov/bcp/edu/pubs/consumer/credit/cre16.shtm.

Chapter 4

GAIN REMOTE ACCESS SECURELY

Today, many companies have what can be considered a mobile workforce. In the name of productivity, many employees need to be able to remotely connect to their company's network. This can include salespeople, insurance adjusters who travel to a client's site, and traveling executives; the list goes on and on. It can even be as straightforward as wanting to be able to access your company's network while working at home. While your business model may require that you can access your computer 24/7, the truth is that most small companies don't have the luxury of having around-the-clock, on-sight employee coverage. The challenge, then, is how to provide the remote access that is so critical in today's business environment while providing an acceptable level of protection for your company's data as well as its computer systems. Larger-sized companies often have their own in-house remote access solutions with a team of computer engineers to help maintain it. However, we are not talking about large companies here. The challenge, then, is to allow employees of small companies to access their network remotely, on a limited budget, and without introducing a significant amount of data security risk.

THIRD-PARTY-PROVIDED REMOTE ACCESS

I want to preface my discussion about remote access software provided by a third party by saying that with data security, you are often faced with choosing between functionality, access, and security. Then, of course, there are also limitations with regard to technical expertise and budgetary restrictions. I believe that the best decisions are always well-informed ones. Depending on your specific business model and the nature of the data with which you are dealing, you may very well be willing to accept a higher level of risk than would a bank or a credit card company, for example. It's also why, in most cases, I am more interested in providing readers with the information necessary to make informed decisions relating to computer security rather than coming right out and condemning certain products or services. Remote access software is no different.

A number of companies provide remote access solutions, all with slight variances regarding pricing and software configuration. One of the most attractive features of a third-party-provided, Internet-based remote access solution is its low cost. While the prices vary from company to company, most charge around $25 or less per month for their service. In general, companies that offer this type of Internet-based remote access service utilize similar methodologies in allowing you to access your remote computer. In most instances, the data travels from your computer over the Internet and then lands on a computer at the company that is providing the remote access service. From there, the data continues on its way on to a computer at your company's network, and of course, back again. This is important, considering that we're talking about Internet-based remote access solutions. As I have previously stated, the Internet is the source of the overwhelming majority of remote hacking attempts. So utilizing this type of remote access solution, will involve connecting your company's computing assets to the Internet. It's also worth asking if your data merely uses their systems as a conduit as it travels remotely between your two computers, or if they maintain copies for any reason. If they store it, it's likely that they're creating copies of it as well. The odds are that they back up their production servers, which includes those that are storing your data.

Protective Measures

Most companies that provide this type of remote access service will encrypt that data as it travels across the Internet. As an example, GoToMyPC.com encrypts data while in transit with a rather strong cryptographic algorithm, Advanced Encryption Standard (AES). This is a very important security feature. There are devices that can look at and even capture data as it travels across network wires. They are actually troubleshooting tools used to help diagnose and resolve data transmission issues. The problem is that, in the wrong hands, these same tools can be used to illegally capture data as well. Encrypting data as it's in transmission will make it unreadable to these type of devices. Aside from encryption, other protective measures can be used as well. For example, some common features include requiring that you enter in a username and password in order to access your computer remotely. Some companies will also require that you provide them with a valid e-mail address. This is not only a convenient way for them to send you promotional updates, but it's also a security feature. It's common practice today for companies to send you an e-mail after the password to your account has been changed. Obviously, if you receive such an e-mail, and didn't change your password, there's a problem. Some companies will allow you to change your password only after you enter in a code that they send to the e-mail account that you provided when you initiated the service with them. That's a nice feature, and it is effective in thwarting hackers from trying to change your password in order to access your account.

Some companies have even gone as far as allowing users to create a list of onetime-use passwords. Onetime-use passwords, which are sometimes referred to as firecall IDs, are generally used when remote access is needed only on an emergency basis. Enabling an engineer to access a system remotely in the case of a system outage is a popular use of onetime passwords. Since they can be used only once, they are considered more secure than passwords that can be used over and over again. In fact, onetime-use passwords are considered nearly impossible to hack.

Moving beyond onetime-use passwords, there's an old saying in data security: Give an engineer (or hacker) physical access to a computer, and they can break into it. There simply is no system so secure that, with the right knowledge and given access and time, a good hacker would not be able to thwart. So, by the nature of their job, computer administrators usually have the knowledge to circumvent most security features that a system may have in place. They are probably the ones supporting the very security features designed to keep hackers out in the first place. It's why large companies spend so much money on housing their servers in data centers that have a myriad of security controls to keep people from being able to gain physical access to them.

One of the last steps is, once in the server room itself, computers are often housed in locked cages. Even people who work in the server room have to go through yet another step to gain actual physical access to a computer. The keys to the cages are usually well guarded, with records kept of who took a key to what systems and when. And, of course, they have to be on an authorized list even to get the keys in the first place. Also, since your data is stored on Internet-aware servers, it is only as secure as their servers are. If their servers are ever hacked, your data could be at risk. Another saying in the data security field is that it's not *if* an Internet-facing server will be hacked, but *when*. It's why large companies usually separate their Internet-facing servers from the rest of their network with a firewall. It's called a demilitarized zone, or simply DMZ.

It is not uncommon for large companies to hesitate to notify their customers about a security breach. They, of course, are concerned about the reputational impact, as well as the business risk, that such a public announcement could potentially have on their company. Companies that provide remote access services would also have to deal with such pressures if they ever suffered a security breach. This is particularly true if the breach involved the loss of customer data. Lots of federal and state-level laws mandate that companies disclose the breach of personally identifiable customer data such as a person's name and Social Security number. Obviously, the impact of this type of event for a company such as GoToMyPC.com would be especially acute, since the company's entire business model is built on their customers using their secure service to access their company computers remotely.

"No Firewalls Please—They're Inconvenient"

Another all-too-common aspect of companies that provide remote access service that I found somewhat disconcerting is how their software deals with firewalls. Many will instruct users to disable or even delete any firewalls that might be employed to protect your home or small business computer network. In my opinion, this is an example of what I've dubbed "lazy engineering." Rather than make the effort to know what "holes" need to be opened to permit their remote access software to traverse a firewall, they will all too often simply ask you to turn it off.

Firewalls are no longer limited to those huge expensive tools used only by large businesses. Current versions of Windows, such as XP and Vista, come with firewall software preinstalled on them. Some people will opt to purchase firewall software, which may very well come bundled in with a suite of protective software. While the number is increasing, most home users do not have a dedicated piece of firewall hardware. However, with the advent of multifunction appliances, even small businesses often have firewalls beyond a piece of software installed on their end-users' workstations. Discussed in greater deal in Chapter 7, a whole host of multifunction security appliances are on the market today that, in addition to acting as a firewall, act as a spam filter, provide antivirus protection, and more. The configuration steps below do not address how to permit the software to traverse a separate hardware firewall.

'Another issue that I found troubling was that some remote access companies actually provide instructions on how to bypass a company's firewall in order to be able to use their service—even if it's against company policy where you work. This speaks to the importance of having computer usage policies, and how certain companies dismiss the fact that some businesses might want to utilize their service.

One well-known company that provides remote access services actually states on its Web site that their services introduce *"no security risk to your company."* Those words concern me. It's simply not true that a remote access service does not introduce any risk to a company's computer network. To be fair, in my 20-plus years in information security, no vendor has ever said that its product would introduce risk into a computer network. They all claim to be risk free or conveniently make no mention of risk at all. The hard truth, however, is that most software, particularly remote access software, does introduce a certain amount of data security risk into a given computer network. Even security appliances, if not configured or maintained properly, can introduce an element of risk into a computer network.

Do Not Mix and Match

If your company utilizes a remote access solution, stick with one and only one. It simply does not make sense to have employees opting to use a remote access solution other than what has been approved and installed on your systems. One of the biggest security risks that a company can have is permitting its employees to "do their own thing." Allowing employees to load any software that they please on company computers can introduce any number of data security risks. Unknown software can also cause compatibility issues, causing computer systems to malfunction. If you plan to allow employees to utilize remote access software, decide on a solution and mandate that all employees use only that one.

Home or Business: Create a List of Approved Software

Working off of an approved list of software can not only reduce your risks, but it can save you money as well. The more "stuff" that you have loaded on your computer network, the harder it is to keep running, and the greater the chance that it won't run altogether. In short, you're increasing your administrative costs by not restricting what software employees can load on their work computers. I will state here that, as with most security measures, it's good to avoid getting overly Draconian. It is common for employees to want to load pictures of family and friends onto their computers, often using them as part of a desktop display. I'm okay with that, as it is certainly less risky than having multiple remote access solutions installed on your employees' workstations. I first started working with computers professionally while serving in the U.S. military. I always keep in the back of my mind that the level of security that is both necessary and prudent depends on the environment in which you are operating. Most of us do not need military-level computer security. That perspective is why I say, let your employees load pictures of their kids and their pets on their workstations.

Perhaps one of the easiest ways to help ensure that your employees (or family members) are not loading unapproved software on either their workstations or laptops is to not grant them the authority to do so in the first place. I have found it dangerous to grant end-users more rights on a computer than they actually need. Grant too many rights to a computer, and you give an end-user the power to cause a level of harm that a repair engineer might not be able to fix. For Microsoft Windows–based servers, the highest level of access is called "Administrator." In the majority of cases, Windows requires a user to have Administrator rights to be able to load software onto a computer. So, by not granting them those rights, you will, in effect, be stopping them from loading unapproved and unknown software on their systems. End-users with a little computer knowledge are often more dangerous than those with none at all. Those with a little computer knowledge will try to "fix" things and that, in and of itself, can cause more problems. You will actually lower your administrative costs by granting your end-users the minimum amount of rights to their computers that they need in order to perform their jobs. For most people, that probably doesn't entail much more than sending/receiving e-mail, writing documents, and creating spreadsheets.

VPN Solutions

A lot of Virtual Private Network (VPN) appliances are available on the market today. They allow users to remotely connect to other computers in a protected or "private" manner. Simply put, the transmissions between the two systems are encrypted to provide a level of privacy. Some products are strictly VPN solution devices, while others have multifunctional purposes, boasting a whole host of network protective abilities.

The obvious question here is, "which one is best for my home office or small business?" I would say that decision, in part, is based on the specific needs of your organization. If you already have a firewall, an antispam filter, and so forth, in place, perhaps an appliance that is strictly a VPN solution would be best. I'm not really a big fan of overlapping solutions for small businesses, as they add a level of difficulty to both maintenance and configuration. If there is an issue, you will have to troubleshoot multiple solutions and work with the different vendors in trying to address the issue. That said, if you are just building out the computer network for your business and wondering about firewalls, VPNs, spam filters and antivirus, a multifunction appliance would probably be just fine. Not only is a single multifunction device cheaper than numerous solutions, but in the event of an issue, you would have the added benefit of having only a single vendor to call for help. A word of caution here: A single device also means a single point of failure. If the device fails, your entire network could be seriously impacted. The solution, of course, would be to purchase a spare, and have it preconfigured and ready to use in the event your primary device were to fail. Companies such as SnapGear, SonicWall, and Juniper Networks all offer such multifunction devices.

CLIENTLESS VPN SOLUTIONS

A slick way to reduce your hardware costs and increase your ability to VPN (yes, it can be used as both a noun and a verb) into your network from any Internet aware computer is to go clientless. That means the solution does not need you to have any "client" software loaded on your PC when trying to VPN into your business's computer network when you are working from the coffee shop. As is true in most instances, with increased flexibility comes a certain amount of risk. Unknown computers carry with them an unknown amount of risk. You don't know how they are configured, if they are full of viruses, if they have spyware loaded on them that's recording your keystrokes, or any other of a host of hacker evils that may reside on them. That said, going clientless is certainly more convenient. Aside from "anywhere" VPN access, you won't have to purchase laptops for all of your employees who may need to access your network remotely. If your employees are not carrying their work laptops with them, then obviously those devices can't be lost or stolen, either. That is yet another advantage. This is very important from a data security perspective, considering the number of high-profile data breaches that have involved lost or stolen laptops. If your company doesn't deal in sensitive information, and you're not worried about a data breach, there's always the cost of having to replace lost and stolen laptops. At around $1,000 a piece depending on the model, merely from a cost avoidance perspective, the fewer laptops that you have to replace, the better.

INSTANT MESSAGING

I am continually amazed by just how much technology has changed our perceptions of communication. If you have been on Earth long enough, you will remember when only doctors carried pagers, and they were strictly for medical emergencies. Later, yuppies carried them as well, as a way to demonstrate just how cool and hip they were. The pager was quickly pushed aside with the advent of the cell phone. In the United States today, probably more people over (and under) age 18 have cell phones than not. I will never forget the first time I saw a young boy riding a skateboard while chatting on his cell phone. I'm sure today that he is talking on his cell phone while driving. Not to be left behind, the technologies surrounding written communications have also seen rapid changes. Ask yourself just how many kids in high school today have never even seen a typewriter or know what correction fluid ("white-out") is. For a time, e-mail was deemed the top in its class as it provides for near-real-time transmission of messages and attachments. What was measured in days with traditional mail became measured in minutes or even seconds, depending on the speed of the computer network.

However, near-real time apparently wasn't quite fast enough; hence, the invention of instant messaging. Demonstrably quicker than e-mail, instant messaging is about as instantaneous as our current state of technology will permit. Not only is it quicker than e-mail, but instant messaging also pops a window up on your computer screen—a real attention getter. So, while you might not see that important e-mail that just arrived in your inbox, an instant messaging window in the middle of your computer screen is hard to miss. A technology that had not even been conceived of 20 years ago is now deemed business critical by many companies. I recognize that knowledge is power, and the faster that ideas can be shared, the better. However, as is all too often the case with computer technology, with convenience comes a certain degree of risk.

ONLINE INSTANT MESSAGING

Companies such as Yahoo, MSN, AOL, Google Talk, and more all offer Internet-based Instant Messaging. Most of these solutions are free to download, thus providing a low-cost or, at times, even no-cost instant messaging solution. These free solutions come with some downsides, however. Think of an Internet-based instant messaging solution as a party line for telephones in years past. Assume that others will be able to read what you are writing. If it is potentially sensitive in nature, think twice before discussing it on an Internet-based instant messaging chat session. Also bear in mind that hackers can exploit Internet-aware instant messaging software as an access point into your computer network.

There is also the lost productivity issue here as well. Do you want your employees spending their time chatting with people on-line or working? While I don't have hard statistics on this issue, just as employees play solitaire and Minesweeper, many will IM on-line, as well, given the chance. That free online instant messaging solution just got a little bit more expensive.

KIDS AND INSTANT MESSAGING

It's a personal decision to decide when your son or daughter is old enough to use instant messaging to "chat" with friends. While Chapter 11 goes into much greater detail on this, Internet-based instant messaging can expose your children to online predators. To a level you feel is appropriate for your children, speak to them about "stranger danger." It's not just the unknown adult hanging around the schoolyard today; it's also the unknown name on the other end of that instant messaging session. A good rule of thumb is to insist that your kids IM only with people they know in the "real world." This would include their school buddies, teammates, fellow band members, etc.

SECURE INSTANT MESSAGING

On a more positive note, there are ways to realize the value in the near-instantaneous communication capabilities of instant messaging while reducing your risks. The truth is that instant messaging is a slick tool. I have used it many times myself while on conference calls to "chat" with other attendees to resolve questions in real time as they come up. The most secure way to have an instant messaging capability within your company is to keep it strictly within your company. This would be opposed to using any of the common Internet-based online instant messaging services such as the ones that I've listed above. I do not mean to denigrate any of the aforementioned online services, as they certainly do have their place. It's just that, as with many solutions, they have their pros as well as their cons.

Some companies sell instant messaging software that is designed to be used with the confines of your company. Companies such as WireRed and Jabber sell instant messaging solutions that are designed for use within a given computer network. An interesting feature with Jabber is that it is also compatible with many of the Internet-based instant messaging solutions. So, you can securely instant message internally with coworkers, yet also be able to instant message with people who are on other solutions such as Google Talk, AOL, etc. While that reintroduces the risk of instant messaging with people over the Internet, depending on your business model, it may be a risk that you are willing to accept. It would still provide greater protection for your employee to employee internal instant messaging.

In addition to enabling businesses to reduce or even eliminate the risk of instant messaging over the Internet, both of these solutions can also maintain a log of the instant messages that your employees are sending to each other. Such a log may be very helpful to you and your company in the event that one employee accuses another of sending inappropriate messages that may be construed as sexual harassment via instant messaging. With a log containing all the sent messages, it will go beyond a "he said, she said" and will go to prove or disprove such allegations. This is beyond the moral duty of wanting to protect employees from harassment, and goes straight to your liability as either a manager or owner of the business. If you become aware of a sexual harassment complaint and fail to act upon it, you have just opened yourself up to a lawsuit. Having a record of the allegedly inappropriate instant messages can make your next decisions much easier.

MEETING SOFTWARE

Depending on how technically savvy your business is, you may want to enhance your conference-calling experience by actually being able to allow attendees to see what you are doing on your computer. This can be much more informative than strictly trying to verbalize certain concepts or even reading off of a static presentation sent out prior to the meeting. With this type of visualization software, as the presenter, you can demonstrate a product that you are trying to sell, or permit for real-time collaboration among coworkers to edit documentation that is a work in progress. As with both e-mail and instant messaging, there are solutions that are Internet-based as well as those designed for use within the confines of your company. As with the other Internet-based solutions, with the convenience comes a certain degree of security risk. It's important to bear in mind that you're actually sharing a portion—if improperly configured, a very large portion—of your computer files with meeting attendees over the Internet. It may well be that most Internet-based teleconferencing software requires attendees to enter a password provided by you, the meeting organizer; that said, however, nothing stops them from sharing it with others.

Most companies that offer this type of solution have wording on their Web sites that state that data being sent over the Internet to the attendees is always encrypted. I am somewhat skeptical of that claim when I read on several providers' Web sites that their software can traverse a firewall by either port 443 or port 80, whichever responds first. Secure Socket Layer (SSL) is the current de facto encryption standard for transmitting data over the Internet in an encrypted form. When a Web site begins with HTTPS, it is in fact using SSL (as denoted by the "S" at the end of HTTP). By default, SSL traverses a firewall using port 443. The other de facto port used for transmitting data over the Internet is port 80. Unlike SSL, port 80 data transmissions are not encrypted. With a Web site that begins with HTTP (no "S") you are transmitting data in the clear (unencrypted). So, if the solution you are using for Internet-based teleconferencing can transmit data over port 80, those transmissions are very likely going to be sent without encryption. That is not to say you shouldn't use Internet-based meeting software; rather, just be cognizant of the potential risks.

There is software that will allow for this type of real-time meeting collaboration that is not Internet-based. Microsoft NetMeeting is one that is commonly used. It is important to denote the difference between Internet-based and Internet-capable. With NetMeeting, you can limit the audience to individuals within your company or trusted third parties that have a secure connection to your organization. However, you can also allow people that participate in a NetMeeting who will connect over the Internet. Again, similar risks will be involved just as with Internet-based solutions. NetMeeting also has the option to transmit data utilizing encryption, if you choose to enable that feature. It's a configuration that you can control and make mandatory to protect your data while it's in transit. It's not optional, as with many Internet-based teleconferencing programs.

Perhaps one of the biggest risks with this type of software is the presenter not configuring it correctly. The whole precept behind live collaborative software is that it allows you to share a program on your computer with others for either demonstrative or illustrative purposes. The responsibility resides with you as the presenter to share only what you want attendees to see. In most cases, that means checking the box of the program you want to share, and nothing else. A common mistake is to over-share, thus putting your computer's data at risk. This risk goes beyond hacking. It could be embarrassing to share e-mails or other programs that are supposed to be confidential with people attending a collaborative conference call. NetMeeting also has an option to allow attendees to take control of the presenters' program. That particular feature must be enabled by the presenter. It may be a feature that you want utilized based on business need. Since granting a person control of applications located on your computer can entail a certain degree of security risk, my recommendation is that you use it only as needed.

FILE AND PRINT SHARING

A functionality that is native to the various forms of the Windows operating system is the ability to share both the files on your computer as well as the printer that you're connected to with others. A simple rule of thumb is that if you do not regularly share files with coworkers or family members, then don't enable file sharing. Also bear in mind that in this day and age, it is just as easy to e-mail somebody a file that they need without having to actually grant them access and share it on your computer. There are a number of issues with enabling file sharing on a computer. First, it assumes that for either your home or small business network, your coworkers know how to connect to your computer. Since end-user workstations are not generally shared network resources, it will take a number of configuration settings to prepare the file on the computer so that it's available with those who need access. Once you have cleared that hurdle, it's important that you share only the files that you intend to share. Accidentally share more, maybe including even your entire hard drive, and you expose other information on your computer to improper disclosure. Of course, if your computer is also connected to the Internet, read improper disclosure as hacking.

It is also common to want to share a printer with coworkers or family members. It's also much less expensive to be able to share a printer wherever possible than to purchase printers for each and every employee in your company. As with file sharing, it is possible to share a printer that is connected directly to an end-user's workstation with others on the same network. Again, if that computer is also connected to the Internet, there is a security risk involved in doing so. Also bear in mind that a shared printer that's connected to an end-user's workstation will be available to others only if both the printer *and* the workstation are powered on. If a coworker is out of the office due to illness or vacation, and their computer is turned off, the office printer that is connected to their workstation will be unavailable. In the name of both computer security and resource availability, consider connecting the shared printer to a server a router or another type of networking device.

Servers are designed to act as a shared resource. At a macro level, servers are generally considered more secure than most end-user workstations. Whatever engineering support a small business might have will generally be more focused on the larger shared resources, such as servers, than on individual workstations and laptops. Support personnel will have the passwords to access the server, while not necessarily being able to access everybody's personal workstations. Servers are also of a higher grade of hardware than workstations and hence are better able to deal with the demands of being on for extended periods of time. It is not uncommon for servers to be powered on around the clock for months or even years at a time. It will also save your company money by powering off workstations when employees go home for the day, or are out of the office. Such a measure is not possible when their workstation is acting as the office printer server.

Computers on a network are also connected by one or more centralized resources depending on the size of the network itself. If the shared printer is connected directly to a networking resource, such as a router, hub, or switch, it can be shared with other computers that are on the same device. As a centralized networking resource, they are not tied to a single end-user and will not be impacted when that one person is out of the office. Connecting a printer to a centralized networking resource will make it available without exposing any single workstation to the additional data risks of acting as the print server.

iTunes

One of the current rages is listening to music by way of software such as iTunes. Many devices from Apple can listen to iTunes music. Odds are that Apple has a device out there to meet your music listening needs. With iTunes, there is also the ability to share your music with others. When originally released, it was possible to share your iTunes music with others over the Internet. That functionality was removed with the release of version 4.1 back in 2003. While this was done to protect sales of iTunes music, Apple actually plugged a security hole by not allowing file sharing over the Internet. The ability to share iTunes music was intended to be among friends and family, and not with anybody who has access to the Internet.

Today's versions of iTunes still allows for such sharing, just not over the Internet. It actually reminds me of the whole issue with another music-sharing application called Napster. It, too, used to allow for the free sharing of music files with anybody over the Internet. Aside from the security implications of sharing files on your computer with anybody who is online, lawsuits were filed to protect the copyrights of the songs that were being so freely copied. While untold millions of copies of songs were made during that time, you do not see free Internet-based music sharing today. Today, you need to purchase songs that you want to download off of the Internet.

Internet File Sharing

Even after the lawsuits involving Napster, programs are still available today that allow users to share their music files (iTunes, MP3) and more. Limewire and KaZaA are two popular examples of file-sharing programs. Both are available for free download from their respective Web sites. They allow users to share their files with others over the Internet. In order to share your computer files with a remote user, the other user must have the same program installed on their computer. Just as you can allow others to copy your files, you can download files that remote users have shared as well. A word of caution: If you inadvertently share your entire computer hard drive, remote users will be able to copy everything that's on your computer. That includes your tax records, your family's medical information, your will, the passwords needed to access your online banking—everything. The risks to any personal information that you have on your computer is enormous.

The risks of Internet file sharing are not limited to data loss. There's also the real possibility of downloading a computer virus. Now, the both Limewire's and KazaA's Web sites state that they attempt to filter out viruses and other harmful programs. The truth is that while the attempts might be admirable, they certainly can't be foolproof. The fact is that in addition to data loss, you are exposing your computers to problems that—if you're lucky—your antivirus will be able to fix.

As much as a risk of file sharing and being online can be when connected via a network cable (a wire), the risks are even greater when going wireless. While certainly more convenient than being tethered to a piece of cable, it does introduce some interesting security challenges. Let's talk about them and how to better protect yourself when going wireless.

Chapter 5

Keep Hackers and Snoops Out of Your Wireless World

The advent of the wireless network is arguably one of the greatest technological advances of the computer age from an ease-of-use perspective. Instead of being tethered to a network cable, we are now free to cruise along on the Information Superhighway from just about anywhere. This freedom has gone beyond just being merely convenient to being downright hip and even cosmopolitan. From teenagers to retirees, places ranging from the local Starbucks to Internet cafés are full of people drinking lattes while accessing the Internet wirelessly.

As is true with most conveniences involving computing and access to data in electronic form, wireless networking brings with it a certain amount of risk.

Protecting Your Home Wireless Network

Being able to take advantage of wireless networking at home is great. Instead of being tethered to a length of network cable, people can work on their computers while sitting in their backyard next to the pool. As with portable radios, computers react very badly when they get wet, so don't work too close to the pool. Aside from the "keep it dry" piece of advice, there are other things you can do to protect your home wireless network. While my main focus here will be on small businesses, much of the same advice applies to home wireless networks as well.

Wi-Fi, Wi-Fi Everywhere

Wi-Fi services are popping up all around us. More and more cities across the country are starting to offer free wireless services. Whether intended more for the convenience of the residents, or as a tool to attract tourists, local governments are hopping on the Wi-Fi provider bandwagon. It's not uncommon for airports to have Wi-Fi hotspots. Many, although certainly not all, are free of charge. Hotels have been offering Internet access for years. In my travels, some hotels offer wireless connectivity, while others have the cabled or "wired" variety, and still others offer both. Some hotels charge a fee for the Internet access they offer, while others provide it for free. Airports and hotels recognize that a good many travelers are in fact businesspeople, and offering Internet connectivity is quickly becoming an expected service rather than a luxury.

BECOMING A WIRELESS HOTSPOT

Yet another popular niche in the Wi-Fi market is that of the Internet café. Does your business want to become a "Wi-Fi Hotspot" to help attract customers? Actually, if you are an upscale coffee house, not having wireless for your customers can be bad for business. More and more people are expecting to be able to go online while having a business lunch, the morning bagel, or that mocha latte. If you are the proprietor of a local eatery or coffee house that is not online, chances are most of your competitors are, and that is not good for your business.

Offering this convenience does come with some drawbacks. First of all, of course, there are costs involved in being a wireless hot spot. The local Internet service providers (ISP) are not going to hook you up for free. Exact setup fees and recurring monthly pricing will vary from ISP to ISP, and will also vary depending on where in the country you are located and the kind of network speed (capacity) that you want to have. The greater the speed, the faster the performance will be for your customers, and the more customers that you will be able to have online at the same time.

It is also important to note that in most cases, you are not going to be able to charge customers for using your wireless network. That is because the market will not support that business model. If your competition is offering *free* wireless Internet access, your customers are not going to be willing to pay for it at your place of business. As mentioned, it is quickly becoming an expected feature in many business categories. Coffee houses charging customers for wireless Internet access have faded away into history just like the old pay toilet did.

A FREE LUNCH

We have all heard the old adage in business that says, "there's no such thing as a free lunch." However, there is such a thing as people using the free wireless Internet connectivity that you have installed for your customers without buying lunch. It is very common for people to visit wireless hot spots to gain free Internet access with no intention of actually ordering that cup of coffee or buying a meal. *Nothing for me, thank you. I'm just here to use the Internet.* I kind of think of it as noncustomers wanting to use your business's bathroom. I actually have more sympathy for those people, because the truth is we all have to use the bathroom, but we could all live without wireless Internet (no matter what your children may claim). This is especially true when traveling with small children.

That said, it is possible to control access to the wireless Internet service your business offers, just like the bathrooms that are for use by your customers. However, to do so, you are going to need something other than a brass door key on a big clunky key chain. There are technical controls that can help block the "free lunchers" from using your company's Wi-Fi service. I also believe that such technical controls are safer (not to mention better for business) than physically challenging people in your place of business that are using your Wi-Fi without buying anything.

Access Control

A way to combat the free Wi-Fi Web surfer crowd is to require people to type in a password or a PIN in order to access your wireless Internet connection. Many wireless network providers offer a service that brings up a Web page requiring users to enter a password when they first use their Web browser. To gain full Internet access, they must enter the correct password. This, of course, means that you will need to be able to give the password to your customers easily. There are a number of ways you can do that. It can be printed on receipts if your establishment requires people to pay first, such as in most coffee houses. You could have your wait staff tell your customers what the Internet password is upon request. From there, you would change your password at a frequency that suits your needs. If you starting to see free lunchers hanging around, it might be a good time to change that password.

I have heard detractors say that any kind of inconvenience for customers outweighs the security benefits. It is up to you as the business owner to know your customers and their tolerances for being required to enter in a password to use your free wireless Internet. There is also a marketing opportunity here, and that also depends on the makeup of your customer base. People who work in industries that deal in information that is heavily regulated, for example, are quickly becoming ever more aware of data security issues. If your business is located in a financial district, your customers could very well appreciate the extra level of security that you're integrating into your Wi-Fi service.

CUSTOMER SAFETY

A common hacker trick is to set up rogue wireless access points to trick people into using their service instead of a legitimate service. When connected to the hacker's rogue wireless, customer data is vulnerable and can be stolen. Hackers can also plant a virus, a "Trojan" (which, just as the name entails, is harmful software hidden inside a legitimate program) or other malware that will either damage computers or snatch data that will be sent back to the hacker at a later time. The Internet café that first sends their customers to a login Web page will help ensure that their customers are accessing their wireless service, and not that of a rogue hacker. As a business owner, you can promote this as caring for your customers by providing this level of security for them.

REMOTE WORKING—WIRELESSLY

The freedom of being able to connect to the Internet without being tethered to a cable goes beyond convenience and directly to increased productivity on the job. In the twenty-first century, if you are not using wireless as a traveling executive, an insurance adjuster, a salesperson, or any one of multiple other mobile occupations, you are at a real disadvantage. This is especially true when you consider that most of your competitors use wireless technologies frequently. At a macro level, people work remotely with their mobile computers in two main ways. The first is for users to just enter data locally on their laptops, so then it can be uploaded to the appropriate company computers when they get back into the office. It is not uncommon to see people responding to e-mails from their laptop while traveling on airplanes. Their e-mails do not actually go anywhere at that point; rather, they just sit in the outbox until they can connect to their company's network again at some later time. While the outbound e-mails aren't actually delivered, this type of queuing up does allow the traveling worker to be productive even while off-line. A fair amount of this book was written in airport terminals and while flying for my day job.

The second way in which people use their laptops in "anywhere" mode is by remotely accessing their company's computer systems while they are away from their office by using wireless. The first scenario carries with it a much lower degree of risk due to the fact that data is not actually being sent streaming across the airways. Now let's talk about how to safeguard data when utilizing the second scenario. In this scenario, users are actually connecting to their company's computer network remotely. This means that data being sent through the air (wireless) and over the Internet on its journey from a user's computer to the systems located at their company's network.

Virtual Private Network (VPN)

As mentioned in the last chapter, many companies have virtual private networks (VPNs) to allow their employees to access the network remotely from anywhere they can access the Internet. As wireless coverage is getting more and more comprehensive, soon you will be able to work remotely from almost anywhere. I have no doubt that we'll see the day when the Phantom Ranch, located on the bottom of the Grand Canyon, goes online. (But I wouldn't necessarily want to carry my laptop with me as I'm hiking down the canyon.) A VPN will, in fact, protect the confidentiality of data while it is in transit from your laptop to your company's computers. It is important to note however that VPNs do not protect the data that is housed on your laptop. This is because there is a difference between protecting data in transit, which is what VPNs can do, and protecting data at rest on a computer's hard drive, which they cannot do. Encryption protects the confidentiality of data. While certainly not an end in itself, encryption certainly does go a long way to keeping data from falling into the wrong hands. In fact, a number of fine products on the market today will encrypt the data that your traveling workforce has stored on their laptops. Chapter 9 goes into greater detail about the different types of encryption solutions that are available to help protect your data.

VPN Architectures

If your company is going to offer remote access for its employees, VPNs are a good way to protect data while in transit. Of course, this can be accomplished in many different ways. I recommend that your company invest in its own VPN architecture. For small businesses, that could be as simple as purchasing a multifunction device that includes a VPN capability. There are devices today that can act as a combination firewall and VPN appliance. Smaller ones, with a capacity of up to 10 concurrent VPN connections, cost less than $400. While you should certainly check, most come with either online or telephone support to help you with installation. Once properly installed, you would be able to connect to your business computers remotely for as long as you had access to a computer with an Internet connection. This way, you will be able to maintain control over how it is used and what level of security you are comfortable with. For example, it is common for VPN "tunnels" to terminate and have the data transmission decrypted at a point just on the inside of a company's network before allowing traffic to proceed on to other systems. This design allows any security monitoring software to be able to scan a remote user's data transmission. If the data transmissions were to be fully encrypted end to end, such monitoring would be blocked. This is important when you consider that the majority of data breaches are internal. Yes, our own employees are our greatest risk. If you gave them an encrypted VPN tunnel end to end, a rogue employee would be able to steal data under the cover of encryption. Forcing decryption points allows intrusion detection sensors you have installed on the network to monitor what data is leaving your company.

Perhaps maintaining your own VPN solution is not within your business model. You may not have any computer savvy people on staff, or it may be just a hassle that you don't want to deal with. Maybe it's as simple as wanting to be able to "VPN" into your office at all hours of the night, but you don't want to have to worry about driving in to work to try to figure out why you can't. That's fine. A number of companies offer VPN solutions. There are questions that should be asked prior to signing up a company to be your VPN solutions provider. From a business aspect, there is always the issue of cost. What are the initial sign-up fees? What are the monthly charges? How many people can use the product at the same time? You want to be as productive as you can, so ask about performance levels. Keep in mind that actual speeds are more of a function of your ISP. In this instance, performance levels would be more in the area of the availability of their VPN service. Ask about availability guarantees. You do not want to pay for a service that keeps going down for one reason or another or provides a frustratingly poor level of performance. If you do want to be able to VPN in at all hours of the day and night, make sure that the company offers 24/7 support.

Whether your company opts to have its own VPN solution or has contracted with a third party to provide that service, I highly recommend maintaining a degree of control and oversight. I also strongly advise against allowing employees to seek out and use their own VPN solutions. At a minimum, having, for example, 100 employees with 101 different VPN solutions can make for a computer administration nightmare. There are sure to be any number of compatibility issues with other software on the laptop. Now, consider having to pay computer engineers to resolve such compatibility issues with 101 different VPN solutions. That can get expensive quickly.

Stopping employees from installing and using their own VPN software on their work computers is as simple as restricting their user rights. Instead of giving them Administrator rights on their laptop or workstation, reduce them to a "limited" user. To do this, go to User Accounts on Control Panel and change your employees' accounts from Administrator to Limited. They'll still be able to perform their necessary work functions, but they won't be able to install programs on their computers. It's a good practice in general to restrict Administrator accounts, anyway. As a rule of thumb, if you don't need to install new programs, add or delete user accounts, or make system-wide configuration changes to the computer, then you don't need to be an Administrator on it.

Another issue is that there are VPN products on the market today whose creators have, in my opinion, questionable ethics. A solution that advertises that it allows your employees to bypass any controls your company has in place to block unauthorized software as well as visit prohibited Web sites is not something you want installed on an employee's laptop. Would you encourage employees to thwart company firewalls and software restrictions? I strongly suggest that you insist that your employees use only the VPN solution that your company has tested, purchased, and approved. I also recommend that you have policies that either forbid the loading of unapproved software on company computers or place serious restrictions on such practices. Having such policies promotes awareness of the expectations that you have of your employees and their computer usage. Such policies are also valuable since security settings are not 100 percent effective. For example, some programs can be installed even if employees are only a "limited" user on their computers. While most programs do require Administrator rights in order to install properly, unfortunately, some do not. You need policies to enforce at an administrative level what you're trying to control at a technical one. I also recommend that you regularly audit what software is loaded on your company's systems, including your employees' laptops. Chapter 7 goes into more detail about solutions that will help you maintain an inventory of approved software and see what software is deployed on various systems throughout your company's network.

Your Company's Wireless Solution

Some companies are opting to use wireless for their employees while at work. One reason is that utilizing wireless removes the need to run network cabling to every employee computer that needs to be on your company's network. This can be a real savings in both parts and labor. At a macro -level, wireless is generally seen as a less secure option than wired. However, it does not mean that you can't put some relatively simple controls in place to help discourage hackers. Keep in mind that some will hack you to steal data or to wreak havoc on your computer network, while others just want the free Internet access. In the case of the latter, some hackers have become so brazen that they will leave chalk marks on the ground outside a business that has unprotected wireless access. This practice is actually called warchalking, and is akin to hobo marks from the early twentieth century. (The hobos used such markings to share important information with their brethren such as a particular place that offered free food or a warning that a certain residence was that of a police officer.) Warchalkers also use their code for more nefarious reasons. They use it alert their fellow hackers where there are easy targets for stealing network traffic.

There are simple things that you can do to help protect yourself, your data, and your network. WEP, as indicated in the bottom symbol of Figure 5.1, denotes that Wireless Encryption Protocol (WEP) is being used. WEP is actually considered a weak encryption algorithm by current standards, and the Wi-Fi Protected Access (WPA and WPA-2) encryption algorithms are considered much more robust and harder to hack. WPA-2 is the current de facto standard and is the stronger of the two encryption solutions. While most hackers will opt to find wireless networks that aren't utilizing any encryption, some may try to hack the weaker encryption algorithms. All things being equal, I recommend using either of the stronger ones. All modern wireless equipment support both WPA and WPA-2, so you're not going to have to spend any extra money for the stronger encryption solutions.

Another common security feature in wireless networks is the ability to preconfigure which computers are allowed access. While there is a certain amount of variance among different equipment providers, some of the most common criterion that you can choose from include computer name, IP address, and MAC address. MAC addresses are values unique to a computer's network interface card. (A network interface card is the piece of hardware the network cable plugs into.) Even computers using wireless often have a network address card and hence will have a MAC address. IP, which stands for Internet Protocol, is a numeric address unique to your computer. An IP address works off of the same theory of having an address on your home, thus enabling mail to be delivered to it. These filters help identify computers that are authorized to use your wireless network. While these steps won't make your wireless network hackproof, it will discourage the opportunistic hackers—the ones looking for either free Internet access or an unprotected wireless network so they can cause mischief just for the sake of doing so. Most dedicated hackers go after large companies either for industrial espionage, social activism, or other such causes considered noble in the hacker's mind. An example would be hacking "Big Oil," because of high gas prices or environmental impact.

Such filters are effective and, along with encryption, can be applied equally to your home wireless network, too. Today, even most lower-end wireless appliances have encryption and filtering capabilities. I have had these types of controls on my own wireless network at home for years, and they

Figure 5.1
Warchalking Symbols

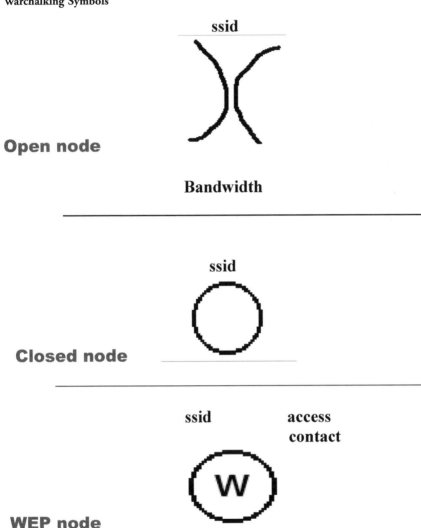

Open node

Closed node

WEP node

work quite well. When I attempted to connect a new laptop recently, I was effectively blocked. Only after I added my machine to the list of accepted systems was I allowed access to my own home wireless network.

WIRED/WIRELESS BRIDGING

A risk to be aware of, and ideally to avoid, is being connected to both a wired network and wireless network at the same time. Most laptops come with wireless capabilities from the manufacturer. While this can be convenient, it can cause the aforementioned wired and wireless (bridging) security problem. The vast majority of laptops that come with wireless capabilities from the manufacturer also have the hardware that allows them to be plugged into a wired network. As I stated above, the particular piece of hardware is called a network interface card, or simply a NIC card. Having a laptop wired into your company's computer network, and at the same time connected to a wireless network has serious security implications.

In the drive to be as end-user friendly as possible, a lot of wireless devices on laptops will try to detect the existence of wireless networks automatically. They can even be configured to look for wireless networks upon startup and continually while powered on. It's akin to real-time antivirus protection. You don't have to do anything; it is always working in the background. When your employees are plugged into your wired computer network at work, you don't want them to also be able to connect to a wireless network at the same time. Consider that your employees' laptops are connected to the interior of your computer network, within the boundaries of any perimeter security you might have, such as firewalls. Now, if those same laptops are connected to wireless networks as well, those wireless networks will be circumventing your firewalls. Wireless goes from the laptop directly into the "air," without wires and without crossing your firewalls. Any hacker who can compromise the wireless network is already on the inside of your network, without having to contend with trying to defeat your firewalls. If your company uses perimeter software to block any Web sites deemed inappropriate by your corporate policies (i.e., pornography, gambling, etc.), those filters will be circumvented as well by wired/wireless bridging.

The solution to this is to configure the wireless software to be disabled when laptops are plugged into a wired network. Most wireless software providers have this capability, and it is one that I strongly suggest you utilize. I would also suggest not using your wireless software's auto-detect feature. Hackers use rogue wireless networks in hopes that laptops will connect to them, enabling them to steal data from your systems. Requiring users to consciously enable wireless, and then join known networks will help defend against inadvertently connecting to a hacker's rogue wireless network.

MODEMS

No discussion about wireless connectivity would be complete without talking about modems. Yes, there are still many modems in use. Modems are, of course, the old standard of connecting to a company's computers remotely over every day-phone lines. For reasons both of data security and of performance, I recommend against using old-style modems. Traditional modems are very slow and will give you a rather frustrating experience trying to send and receive even small amounts of data, not to mention attachments. Traditional modems have a maximum transfer rate in the range of 56K per second. Compare that with cable modems of today that boast speeds ranging from 7 megabytes to over 10 megabytes per second. Today's cable modems, on average, are around 100 times faster than old-style modems. Now, in their day, modems were fine. It's important to keep in mind that old-style modems came into being before the advent of broadband, DSL, and cable modems. Back in their heyday, most people who used modems to transmit data almost always sent only simple text messages. While even that wasn't fast by current standards, at the time, nobody knew any differently, because the faster technologies hadn't been invented yet. An analogy would be that people in the 1800s didn't consider the horse-drawn carriage to be slow. Obviously by today's standards, the old horse and buggy is no match for the speed of automobiles.

From a both a data and computer security standpoint, when the old-style modems were in vogue, the modern Internet hadn't been invented yet, either. When used in the 1980s and even into the 1990s, most modems were used to remotely connect to a single computer or to another network, and not to the Internet. That meant that the would-be hacker would have to try to hack the specific modem transmission rather than "browse" the Internet to try to capture unprotected data transmissions. Old-style modems were also not "always on," as today's DSL and cable modems are. Obviously, when that was the only way your computer transmitted data to other systems, remote hacking was effectively blocked when the modem was turned off. The fact is that most of our technological advances in computing, while a tremendous boon to productivity, have also created opportunities for mischief (hacking) that did not exist pre-Internet and prior to always-on, high-speed connectivity technologies such as DSL and cable. These conveniences aren't bad. Quite the contrary, they have actually given us access to data and a degree of mobility we couldn't even have envisioned 20–30 years ago. It's just that there are those who will try to use this type of ease of use for their own nefarious purposes.

Taking Wireless to the Max: A Look at the Near Future

One of the drawbacks of wireless has always been its range limitations. If your business occupies several floors of an office building, you'll likely need numerous strategically placed wireless access points if you want to allow all of your employees to utilize wireless. Even being a couple of rooms away from a wireless base station can have serious performance implications. This is especially true if the building has thick walls or contains a lot of metal. However, a newer technology called WiMax (Worldwide Interoperability for Microwave Access) has come onto the scene. WiMax is a form of wireless connectivity that offers both greater range and greater speeds than more traditional wireless. WiMax can be used both to connect computer networks as well as for cell phone connectivity. Unlike traditional wireless, WiMax's range is measured in miles instead of yards. Depending on the specific implementation, WiMax can have a range of up to 30 miles. Also, many cities are offering free wireless to its citizens as a convenience. Such a free service will also attract traveling business people and even vacationers. A single installation of WiMax could potentially bring connectivity to an entire city depending on its size.

In addition to its rather impressive range, WiMax also boasts network speeds far in excess of either DSL or cable, with data transmission rates upwards of 75 MB/second. That is very impressive when you consider that common wired network transfer rates run around 100 MB/second. WiMax could be used to connect the networks of two office buildings located within the 30 mile range—say, a business with multiple locations within a given metropolitan area. WiMax could also serve as a backup plan if a company's primary metropolitan area network connectivity were to fail.

The truth is that in whatever form, wireless is here to stay. What will undoubtedly change over time is how we use it. A common saying is that today's science fiction is tomorrow's science fact. Something that wasn't even dreamed of as recently as the 1990s is commonplace today. For instance, wireless Internet to cell phones and PDAs is already a reality. Thumb drives that cost less than $100 have storage capacities that are far greater than entire servers had 10 years ago. I'm certain that today's 30 mile WiMax range will certainly be well over 100 miles in the not-too-distant future. After all, computing technology is one of the fastest evolving technologies that there is.

An unfortunate truth is that while most of us will use all of these incredible devices for their intended purposes, some of us are somewhat less noble. Whether it's clogging our e-mail inboxes with junk e-mail or trying to steal identities for fraudulent purposes, hackers, spammers, and others with mischievous intent are out there. Fortunately, there are simple things that we all can do to help protect ourselves. There's an old saying: "Knowledge is power." So, let's get powerful.

Chapter 6

LAUGH OFF SCAMMERS

As a means of electronic communication, e-mail is perhaps the single greatest invention, second only to the telephone. E-mail is not only quicker than traditional mail—sometimes referred to as "snail mail"—it doesn't cost you a stamp, either. E-mail has given businesses a whole way to communicate at near-real time. It has also made sharing the latest joke with friends all the easier. Unfortunately, as with other technological advances, e-mail has also given rise to those who would use it to communicate for less-than-noble purposes. The advent of e-mail has, in fact, given rise to a whole slew of scams and schemes designed to defraud people in one way or another.

Like most people, I'd love one day just to come into a whole bunch of money. I mean piles of the stuff; millions of dollars so that my first big decision on any given day would be whether to drive my BMW, my Jaguar, or my Lexus. It is the motivating factor behind people who play the lottery—chasing that one-in-a-million chance to strike it rich and to be able to quit your job and "live the good life." However, most of us deep down also realize that short of winning the lottery, the odds of somebody just giving us millions of dollars are somewhat slim, but the desire is still there nonetheless. It is the fact that we have that desire that some tempt us with promises of get-rich-quick schemes that are in reality not-so-veiled attempts to defraud us.

THE NIGERIAN SCAM

They are called Nigerian scams, "4-1-9" scams, and "Advanced Fee Fraud Schemes." This particular type of fraud generally consists of e-mails that, in one form or another, promise us thousands or even millions of dollars for helping somebody move a large amount of money, something they are unable to accomplish on their own. Sometimes, in an attempt to sound even more sophisticated, they'll list some non-U.S. currency as payment. These e-mails are, of course, not legitimate, as nobody is going to give you all that money for doing absolutely nothing. If somebody really had millions of dollars, would they reach out to total strangers and offer them hundreds of thousands of dollars just to help them deposit it in a U.S.-based bank account? Surely, anybody that had millions of dollars would have access to a banker who could perform the work for them for much less. Even if the e-mails were not fraudulent, somebody wanting to give you a ton of money to act as their "banker" should raise some concerns. Why can't they simply go through an established financial institution? Are they dealing in drug money, or some other criminal enterprise? Either way, deep down, we should all know this isn't right. But the fact is, people fall for such scams every day. Just don't let it be you.

With the Nigerian scam, the senders are in fact trying to steal your identity, or fool you into sending them a small transaction fee in exchange for a promised financial windfall. Another common aspect of the Nigerian scam is that the e-mail won't be addressed to you specifically. A more generic salutation of either "sir" or "madam" is commonly used. Since many of these e-mails come from outside of the United States, they'll often be riddled with grammatical errors. I don't mean to assume that only Americans can speak and write English well. My point is that most agencies established enough to be dealing in millions of dollars can afford to hire educated people who would not make such obvious grammatical errors. Since these are, in fact, scammers, they are not as educated and don't even care to use the spell-check feature that comes with most e-mail programs. It is also very common for the e-mails to come from free web-based e-mail accounts. That's even true of e-mails claiming to be from large companies. Below are some examples of actual e-mails, sent to me that promise large sums of money if only I would lend a helping hand.

This first e-mail congratulates me for winning £750,000 in British pounds. You'll note that nowhere does my name appear in the e-mail. While I certainly have nothing against Hotmail, as I said above, most companies dealing with this amount of money have their own e-mail addresses. You wouldn't expect your personal banker to have a work e-mail address on Hotmail, would you? You will also see that the e-mail states that I won a Microsoft promotion. Trust me, Microsoft has its own e-mail domain and doesn't need to use Hotmail accounts to conduct business. Also note that the e-mail originates from one e-mail domain (yyyyyyyy.com—real domain changed) while I'm directed to respond to somebody located on a different one (hotmail.com). Also notice that the "c" in the word "contact" is not capitalized, even though it is the first word in a sentence. Obvious grammatical errors are another sign that the e-mail is a scam. If I were to e-mail this person, I would be asked to provide information where they could send the money—that would include my name and account number, at a minimum. For tax purposes, I would also likely be asked for my Social Security number; that would make it sound more legitimate. Of course, that would also be all the data needed to steal my identity.

From: 0000000@yyyyyyyy.com [mailto:smidgekilty@yyyyyyyy.com]
Sent: Saturday, February 16, 2008 10:35 AM
Subject: Congratulations!! Your Email Id Was Selected
Congratulations!! Your email id was selected and you have therefore been awarded the sum of £750,000GBP by the Microsoft Promotions.
contact this email for further instructions:
00000000@hotmail.com

Thank You

In this next one, a guy that wants me to contact him to help him invest funds. Apparently he can't invest funds in the United States, and needs my help. Okay, do I really want to get involved with somebody who isn't allowed to conduct business in the United States? Even if this wasn't a scam, just what kind of business venture would I be getting myself into? The sender, Mr. Roland Andersson—if that is his real name—states that he has chosen to contact me because I live in a country in which he wants to invest. I was chosen out of the more than 300 million people that live here. If only my luck at the Powerball lottery was that good! Notice that here again, my name isn't mentioned specifically; rather, the salutation is "Sir/Madam" and not directed to me personally. Trust me, there are a lot of other sirs and madams that this person has chosen to receive this e-mail scam.

From: rolandandersson@yyyyyyy.com
Sent: Saturday, February 16, 2008 3:53 AM
To: undisclosed-recipients:;
Subject: Confirm Receipt Asap.

Sir/Madam,

I am Mr. Roland Andersson, and I am contacting you from Dakar, Senegal for a mutual business relationship and investment. I have some funds
realized through contract execution and I need your cooperation to invest the funds. The first
stage requires transferring the funds to your account for subsequent investment. I have chosen to contact you because you live in a country where I want to invest in. I therefore want you to work with me as a partner. On receipt of your response, I will send you full details of the transaction and

more information about myself.
I await your prompt response.

Best Regards
Roland Andersson

This next e-mail is one of my personal favorites. This one was a relatively short e-mail with a Microsoft Word document attached to it, the contents of which also appear below and starts with "My Good Friend." I do happen to be a fan of the 1960s science fiction television series *Star Trek*, so the name *James Kirk* caught my eye. For you non-Trekkies out there, James Kirk is the name of the captain of the Starship *Enterprise* on *Star Trek*. This one actually mentions Nigeria in the e-mail. This guy nails the Nigerian Scam dead on. Apparently, I was helpful in someway in the past, and for my efforts I will be compensated $200,000. Note that as with the other scams, my name is not directly mentioned. Instead, the salutation reads, "Dear Good Friend." Also note how the e-mail isn't addressed to me specifically. The To: line reads, "yyyyyy@gmailo.com." My e-mail address was in the blind carbon copy line, which is why it doesn't show up in the e-mail. It makes you wonder just how many people Captain Kirk sent this e-mail out to.

From: 00000000@gmailo.com
Sent: Saturday, April 05, 2008 9:34 AM
To: yyyyyyy@gmailo.com
Subject: James Kirk

Dear Good Friend,

Sorry for my late response. Check the attached file for update.

Best Regards

James Kirk

(Word document attachment)

My Good Friend,

I'm happy to inform you about my success in getting those funds transferred under the cooperation of a new partner from Nigeria, Africa. Presently I'm in Japan for investment projects with my own share of the total sum.

Meanwhile, I didn't forget your past efforts and attempts to assist me in transferring funds despite that it failed us some how. Now contact Mr. Williams Coky in Nigeria via his E-mail address {rrrrrr@rqlive.com} or call him through his contact phone number +555 555 555 5555 .i left the cheque $200.000 {Two Hundred Thousand US Dollars Only} for your compensation for all your effort and attempts to assist me in this matter. Ask him to send you the cheque that you are the beneficiary.

I appreciated your efforts at that time very much. So feel free and get in touched with Mr. Williams Coky and instruct him where to send the Cheque to you.

Please do let me know immediately you receive it so that we can share the joy after all the suffering at that time. in the moment, I am very busy here because of the investment projects which me and the new partner are having at hand.

Finally, remember that I had forwarded instruction to Mr. Williams Coky to release the cheque to you as the beneficiary as soon as you contact him, so feel free to get in touch with Mr. Williams Coky, he will send the amount to you without any delay.

Why contacting Mr. Williams Coky, include you contact address where he can send the cheque and contact phone number for delivery.

Best Regards,
James Kirk

We all make mistakes, and we have all sent out e-mails containing typos and poor grammar. You'll note that this next one is full of such mistakes. For one, the word *e-mail* is referred to as both email and e-mail. There are also errors in the use of plural vs. singular tenses, and "sweepstakesprogram" is not one word, the last time I checked. Since many scammers are from foreign countries where English is not the primary language, these types of grammatical errors are common. That's yet another indication that the e-mails are not legitimate.

From: Oogla—The Weblog Community
Sent: Sunday, April 13, 2008 11:54 PM
To: Alexander, Philip M.
Subject: Congratulation On Your Winnings!!! NL 2345 BPD Unit!!!!!!!!!!

Oogla—The Weblog Community.
West Way, W76

England,United Kingdom
Lottery Date: 11 April 2008

We wish to inform you of the yearly sweepstakesprogram that your e-mail address has won an award sum of a total cash prize of ONE MILLION BRITISH POUNDS STERLINGS.Xanga lottery is approved to access all registered email address on the internet,so take note that you will not buy a ticket to win in xanga lottery the draws are been played electronically by computer balloting system which randomly select email address arround the world that have been registered since 1995.If your email receive email that you are a winner and you register the email before 1995 then you have been automatically disqualified.

CLAIMS REQUIREMENTS:

1. Name in full
2. Address
3. Nationality
4. Age
5. Sex
6. Occupation
7. Phone/Fax
8. Present Residential Address

For claims Send the requirements to:
Mr Kelvin Thomas
Email:kelvin_thomas44@ZZZZZZZ.co.uk
Phone: +44 555 555 1212
****
Sincerely Yours
R. E. Turner,
Chairman of the Board

(c) 2008 Oogla, All Rights Reserved

In this last one, this person is claiming to be from the Committee of Foreign Payment from the government of Nigeria. Again, I'm not addressed by name, but as you can now see, that's fairly common among such scam e-mails. This one is claiming that I have an overdue inheritance payment. Funny, I've never had any family in Nigeria, so I'm not certain how I would be entitled to receive any kind of inheritance. At least with that last one, I do have some British blood in me. This person is more transparent than the others with the attempt to steal my identity. Notice that I'm asked to provide my banking and personal details as well as my telephone number. This is supposedly to provide evidence that I am entitled to the overdue inheritance. Of course, again, the e-mail wasn't written to me directly, but rather to "Sir/Madam." If there is still any lingering doubt that this e-mail isn't a fraud, I don't believe that the government of Nigeria would use *senatepaymastergeneral@bizhat.com* to conduct official business.

From: info@nastsytnig.org
Sent: Thursday, February 07, 2008 6:58 PM
Subject: OVERDUE INHERITANCE PAYMENT

OFFICE OF THE SENATE HOUSE
FEDERAL REPUBLIC OF NIGERIA
COMMITTEE ON FOREIGN PAYMENT
(RESOLUTION PANEL ON CONTRACT PAYMENT)
NATIONAL ASSEMBLY COMPLEX, ABUJA

OUR Ref: NASS/435/634/AT2008 YOUR Ref:

ATTENTION: SIR/MADAM,

We, the entire members of the Federal House of Senate, on behalf of the Federal Republic of Nigeria, Under the auspices of the new civilian Head of State(President Umaru Musa Yar'adua), held a meeting last week with all Stake Holders involved in your Overdue Inheritance Payment.

The meeting was prior to the Call for Justice by the UN, US and other International Communities involved in this issue and was focused on finding a Lasting solution to all delayed payment both foreign and local contractors and some inheritance funds. This development settling your overdue inheritance funds that has been denied or delayed by corrupt Government official in the past is based on the resolution of the meeting which lasted over eight hours.

Having reached swift agreement, on going through files, we discovered that your file was dumped untreated so at this juncture we apologize for the delay of your payment. Please stop communicating with any office now as we have appointed a liquidator/bank overseas to handle your payment henceforth since our apex bank, the central bank of Nigeria (CBN) has disappointed us in this regard.

Now, all that is needed from you is your BANKING DETAILS,PERSONAL DETAILS,AND YOUR TELEPHONE AND FAX NUMBERS. Re-confirm your contract amount as evidence showing you as the true owner. Send all these above stated information's to the Federation Auditor General through his email thus: senatepaymastergeneral@BBBBB.com His name is Alhaji Nasiru I. Arab.

Also, send a copy to this house for record purposes.

Be rest assured that the Paymaster General of the Federal Republic of Nigeria shall immediately, as soon as he receipt your details as requested above, pay you through a Creditable Bank overseas as a resolution has been passed regarding it by this house. Note that this house is now working hand in hand in making sure that no foul play is played again in the process of paying you.

Contact the above mentioned office now with the details and to avoid complicating our network and the efforts of International Community, the United Nations and the US Government efforts in ensuring a hitch free transfer of your Overdue Inheritance funds to you, please be informed that you are not allowed to correspond to any person or office anymore because you are dealing directly with the Chairman Senate Committee On Foreign Payment Matters in Nigeria EMPOWERED BY THE PRESIDENT FEDERAL

REPUBLIC OF NIGERIA.

We advice you to endeavor to communicate only with the approved office in charge of your payment as we have mounted our security network to monitor every in-coming calls and if we find out that you are still dealing with all those fraudsters that have been frustrating our efforts and defrauding beneficiaries, We shall stop and cancel your payment immediately as an enemy of Nigeria.

David Mark
Senate President

Right about now, many readers are probably thinking that, for the sake of being able to provide such examples, I've done things to attract these types of scams to my home e-mail account. Believe me, that isn't the case. For one thing, all of the e-mails that I've listed were actually sent to my work e-mail account. Even in the spirit of conducting research for this book, I would never visit "questionable" Web sites on company time on my work-issued computer. So, while I didn't do anything to attract all of these scam e-mails, they did prove useful in writing about the Nigerian scams. So, I actually consider them my silver lining in the dark cloud.

THE "RE:" E-MAIL SCAM

We all live very busy lives and forget things from time to time. They've been called "senior moments" and "brain cramps." The list of euphemisms to describe memory lapses that we all suffer now and then goes on and on. The next category of e-mail scams play on those memory lapses. When one replies to an e-mail, e-mail programs will insert "re:" in the subject line. Now, you can simply type "re:" in the subject line and then just add any subject after it; there's no special programming to prevent it. In fact, anybody can simply type "re:" and then a subject, making the e-mail appear to be a reply to something you originally sent to them. The scammers are betting that we'll think that we must have sent them an e-mail, since it appears from the subject line that they are in fact just replying to something that we sent them. In those cases, the act of opening an e-mail can allow malware (Trojans, viruses, worms) to be loaded on your computer. If there's an attachment, opening it would likewise load malware on your computer.

If you don't recognize the sender, think long and hard about opening e-mails. This is particularly true if the senders are from accounts and/or locations that aren't common to what e-mails that you usually receive. In the e-mails that I listed above, not one of them is from an address that I recognize, or is what I would expect to receive on my work e-mail account. Many e-mail programs such as Microsoft Outlook have a preview panel, which enables you to read part of an e-mail without actually opening it. This will let you gather even more information to detect fraudulent e-mails without having to open them. If there is an e-mail in the attachment, don't open it. In many cases, the hacker will hide their viruses and other malware in the attachment. The act of opening it is what will cause your computer to become infected.

If you do suspect that an e-mail is a phony, the best thing that you can do is simply delete it. I've heard some people say that they're tempted to reply to the fraudster and tell them off. For one thing, they really don't care if you send them a strongly worded, condemning e-mail. Depending on their level of technical expertise, they may try to retaliate against you for sending such a response. The best thing that you can do is to just hit delete.

DEFRAUD BY PHONE

Another way that scammers will try to defraud people is by having them call telephone numbers that charge outrageous fees. I'm talking about fees of $50 per minute and more. Imagine between being placed on hold, being switched from one department to another, which would likely be two people sitting right next to each other, being on a call for upwards of 20 minutes, or as long as they could keep you on the line. Multiply that 20-minute phone call by $50 per minute, and they've just defrauded you for $1,000. That's not bad for 20 minutes' work. Since many of these phone scams are located outside of the United States, seeking any kind of legal recourse would be extremely difficult. You're usually left with trying to work with your phone company to not have to pay for the fraudulent charges.

VISHING

Another scam that fraudsters will try to perpetrate by using the telephone is known as vishing. A vishing attack generally consists of the fraudster calling you claiming to be from a credit card company stating that there is something wrong with your account. They will then ask you to provide information about the credit card account. Their goal is to trick you into giving them sufficient information that would allow them to commit crimes such as financial fraud and identity theft. If you ever receive a call that claims to be from your credit card company asking you to provide sensitive account information, hang up. All credit card issuers place a telephone number on the back of their cards that their customers can call with any questions or to resolve any concerns. Hang up on the fraudster, and then call your credit card issuer using the telephone number on the back of your card to verify that everything is okay with your account.

SPAM

I remember when fax machines first made their way onto the scene. Fax paper came in rolls, and was very expensive. Fax spamming occurred when companies would send unsolicited advertisements to your fax machine. A common one was for restaurants to send local businesses their menus and coupons. Helpful information, to be sure, but again, the old-style roll fax paper was very expensive. Fax spam would also tie up your fax machine.

Today, the more common types of spam are those sent via e-mail. At a broad level, there are two types of spammers.

Denial-of-Service Spamming

Unlike the Nigerian scams that try to steal your identity, these denial-of-service spammers are trying to fill up your e-mail servers and clog up your network's transmission lines. The unfortunate truth is that in an attempt to warn coworkers, many will reply to everybody to whom the spammer sent the e-mail with a warning that this is spam. Consider the mathematics of a spammer sending a single e-mail to 100 people in your company. If all 100 employees were to send e-mail warnings to the other 99 advising them of the spam e-mail, that would generate 9,900 e-mails. If the 100 employees then e-mailed the other 99 asking them to stop e-mailing, that you know it's a spam—well you see how this can get out of control very quickly. The best thing to do is to simply delete the e-mail.

Unsolicited Informational Spam

The primary purpose of the other kind of spam is to try to sell you something. Consider it junk mail for your computer. It generally doesn't target large numbers of employees in a company since it's not intentionally trying to slow down a network. The inconvenience of this type of spam is that it's a waste of your good time.

BLOCKING SPAM E-MAILS

Many firewalls are sophisticated enough to be able to block e-mail domains. So, if your company was just hit by "@spamme-mail.com" you could simply block all e-mails coming from that domain. Now, I realize that there are literally hundreds of thousands of e-mails domains out there. This type of domain blocking will not stop all spam. However, it is a relatively simple solution, and will reduce the overall spam that you receive. You can also opt to block an entire e-mail domain instead of one e-mail address at a time; "*@e-maildomain.com" will block every e-mail from "e-maildomain.com." The asterisk ("*") is read by the computer as "anything from." Now, that isn't practical for Hotmail or Yahoo type accounts, as most of us wouldn't want to block every e-mail from such accounts, but it is effective to block entire groups from obvious fraudster e-mail communities. Many e-mail software programs, such as Microsoft Outlook, have a "blocked senders list." It allows you to block e-mail from certain accounts to stop receiving spam. You can add entire e-mail domains as well.

ANTISPAM SOFTWARE

You can always augment the blocked-senders feature native to most e-mail programs by adding an antispam program. Look for those that maintain a list of known spammers and scammers. You want to block not only the annoying solicitations, but also the attempts to steal your identity. Some will even place a folder within your e-mail program so you can see which e-mails are being blocked from your "inbox." You actually want this feature, so that you can check the list from time to time. Software programs do make mistakes, and with antispam, you might not be getting e-mails that you actually want to receive. Generally, programs have some sort of "known sender" or "approved sender" function that will tell the antispam program that it shouldn't block a particular e-mail address. It's also a simple matter to mass-delete the spam e-mails from people whom you don't know. That's much easier than having to filter through your inbox and delete the spam e-mails one at a time.

MY FRIEND JUST SPAMMED ME

So, now that you've just blocked "@spammer_e-mail.com," you received a spam e-mail from somebody you know. In reality, your friend or coworker did not actually spam you or send you a scam e-mail. A common trick is for spammers and scammers to try and access your personal address list. This way, they can make it look like the e-mail came from a known—and trusted—source. This is where the preview feature of many e-mail programs such as Outlook becomes useful. This would also be a possible indication that somebody has managed to get their hands on the e-mail addresses of some of your friends and coworkers. The best thing to do is to just delete the e-mails. Spammers generally don't stick around long, and they'll move on to their next target.

"HAPPY VALENTINE'S DAY!"

Fraudsters don't take holidays. Just the opposite. They will use popular holidays to help them try to commit their mischief. For example, how many of us receive e-mails during a given holiday wishing us Merry Christmas, Happy New Year, Happy Valentine's Day, etc. The fraudsters know this, and will send out e-mails stating that you can pick up your holiday e-card of good cheer by clicking on a hyperlink. Once you've clicked on their hyperlink, any number of things can happen. The link will actually install malware on your computer that they can use to steal data or just cause mischief and wreak havoc on you computer. If you don't know who the e-mail is from, think twice before clicking on the hyperlink. Most of the common e-card sites such as Blue Mountain are well known. If the link is from an e-card site that you've never heard of, again, think twice. Since I just mentioned how spammers can send e-mails that appear to be from trusted friends and coworkers, when in doubt, ask. If you have doubts about the authenticity of an e-mail that was supposedly sent by somebody you know, ask that person. If it's legitimate, then you can click away.

PHISHING

Another category of scam e-mail is known as phishing. A phishing attack generally consists of an e-mail claiming to be from a bank, a credit card company, or other legitimate business and requiring some sort of action on your part. While the e-mail may claim to be from a bank or other reputable institution, they are, in reality, fraudulent. It is a simple matter for a fraudster to copy the logo of Bank of America, Chase, or other nationally recognized financial institution from their Web site, and place it in their phishing e-mail.

Now, if the link said something like "www.fraudster.com," it wouldn't be very effective. However, it is a very simple matter to edit a hyperlink. So, the hyperlink that would take you to "www.fraudster.com" might actually read "www.ABCbank.com." Carefully placing your cursor over the hyperlink will reveal where it will take you, regardless of what it says. Be careful not to click on the hyperlink, as that will take you to the fraudster's Web site. Now, in a printed book, obviously, there is no risk of accidentally clicking on a fraudster's hyperlink. If you're trying to warn coworkers of such a fraud in an e-mail, deactivate the hyperlink prior to sending on the warning. This way, they won't inadvertently go to the very fraudster Web site that you're trying to warn them about. This can be done by right-clicking on the hyperlink and clicking on "Remove Hyperlink."

Sometimes the fraudsters will get tricky and have their Web site be something like "www.frauderster.com/Bank of America.com." Now, that Web site address does end in "Bank of America.com," so it may, in fact, appear legitimate. The challenge is in knowing how to decipher a hyperlink. In the example above, the Web site is "www.frauderster.com." The part after the slash ("/") is actually a folder on the frauderster.com Web site. The part of the hyperlink that comes before the first .com, .org, .edu, etc., is the true Web site designator; what comes afterwards actually dictates where on the site the particular link will take you.

In the case of a phishing attack, the fraudster will create a phony Web site that will appear to be that of the legitimate business they are trying to impersonate. Some of the hyperlinks on the Web page may, in fact, take you to the real institution's Web site. This will, of course, give the fraudster's site an even higher degree of legitimacy. What the fraudster is trying to do is to get you to provide some kind of information that they can then use to either access your accounts, steal your identity, or both.

The phishing e-mail may state that there is something wrong with your account, and you must log in to address the issue. The link then takes you to their fake Web site, where you'll be prompted to enter in the username and password that you use for online banking. That's it; that's all they need to gain access to your accounts. To keep you from getting suspicious right away, upon typing in your username and password and hitting enter, the fraudster's Web site could return a message saying the site is under maintenance, please try again later. Their site could simply thank you for entering in your account information, and state that the problem has now been resolved, and state that upon closing your Internet browser, you may access your account normally. In essence, the fraudster would be directing you to go to the institution's actual Web site to perform your online banking. Again, this sounds very convincing. This type of attack has been used for banking, credit card accounts, and anything that the fraudster can do to try to either access your money or steal your identity.

If there's really a problem with your account, your bank isn't just going to send you an e-mail directing you to go to their Web site. In most cases, they will call you, or send you a letter in the mail. If they do send you an e-mail, it will include a phone number for you to call. A bank isn't going to try to resolve an issue that one of their customers is having by simply directing them to their Web site.

If there's a doubt in your mind as to the validity of the e-mail that is supposedly from your bank or credit card issuer, the simplest thing to do is to call them. Do not use the phone number provided on the e-mail. If it is a phishing attack, you'll be calling the fraudster. You can call your credit card company very easily, since it always puts the telephone number on the back of its cards.

"I'D NEVER BE TRICKED BY A PHISHING ATTACK"

"It couldn't happen to me; I'm far too smart to fall for a phishing scam." That type of mind-set has led to a specific type of phishing attack known as whaling. Like the name would lead one to believe, whaling is phishing, only going after much larger prey. Whalers are, in fact, targeting very senior people in a given company, or other famous people of high wealth. They are counting on both ego and embarrassment that may cause their victims not to admit that they've been duped. The "rich and famous" also generally have more in their accounts than the rest of us do, making access all the more lucrative for the whaling fraudster. A common whaling technique is for the fraudster to send an executive an e-mail purporting to be from the Better Business Bureau about an investigation. The e-mail will often contain a zip file or other kind of attachment. The executive opens the attachment, which installs malware on the executive's computer. This malware can steal information, make the computer malfunction in one way or another, or both.

Fortunately, there are things we can do to help defend ourselves from becoming victimized by fraudsters, spammers, and hackers. There is software and hardware on the market today designed to help protect both computers and computer users from the dangers that exist. While large corporations employ many highly complex and expensive tools, products are available on the market today that will help the small or home-based businesses, or simply the home computer user. These products offer pretty good protection at reasonable prices. Most are easy to use and come with default settings, technical support, or, in most cases, a combination of both.

Chapter 7

EMPLOY HELPFUL SOFTWARE AND SAFETY TOOLS

Most people know that they need to have some sort of protection for their computers and, more importantly, the data that is stored on them. Even the most novice computer user has a certain amount of awareness of issues such as computer viruses and e-mail spam. The challenge of course, is to know what products are best. Obviously, "best" is a subjective determination. It could mean which products offer the most comprehensive protection, or are the easiest to administer, the most reliable, or even the least expensive. Ideally, the right combination of all of the above to meet your specific needs is what is best for you and your particular situation. I've often heard it said that you can get a product delivered that is good, fast, or cheap—pick two. For large organizations with thousands of employees and huge multistate computer networks, there are no good, fast, and cheap solutions that will offer comprehensive protection for their systems. However, here again, we're talking about home computers, and small businesses. The good news is that there are, in fact, very straightforward solutions that will offer a reasonable amount of security without breaking the bank, and without requiring that you have an advanced degree in computer science.

YOUR INTERNET SERVICE PROVIDER (ISP) TO THE RESCUE

The majority of smaller computer networks, whether they are home or small-business systems, access the Internet through an Internet Service Provider (ISP). Generally speaking, the kind of protective services that ISPs offer fall into one of two categories. One category is that in which an ISP offers a suite of protective software for Internet customers. In most cases, your ISP will offer the suite of software either for free or at a discounted rate. This software suite generally includes some combination of the following: antivirus, anti-spyware, anti-phishing, parental controls, a software firewall, and identity theft protection. While a glossary at the end of the book discusses these terms, here's a quick explanation.

Most of us know, or have an idea of, what a computer virus is. At a high level, viruses can cause computers to lose performance or even not work at all if the "infection" is bad enough. Spyware, as the name entails, is software designed to spy on us. Sometimes it's as benign as simply trying to track where we go on the Internet to determine our online shopping habits. The company that loaded the spyware on the computer would then use that information to bring us offers that attempt to entice us to purchase things online that we've showed an interest in based on observed browsing habits. Phishing, as discussed in the previous chapter, are those fake e-mails masquerading as legitimate offers trying to steal our identities, gain access to our online bank accounts, or have us pay up-front fees for promised millions. Bad stuff, any way you look at it.

Just as one would think, the parental control software allows parents to filter out Web sites that contain content that they don't want their children to see. Internet Explorer, Microsoft's Web browsing application, also has a parental control filtering capability. My personal recommendation is to use one or the other, but not both. For one, it's double the work to configure both filters. Also, there may be times when it would be appropriate to permit access to a Web site that would normally be blocked by a parental control filter. You would have to clear both programs in order to gain access to the particular site. Again, it's up to you and your personal feelings on such matters. Perhaps a dual-layered safety net is appropriate to meet your particular needs.

Unlike dedicated hardware firewall appliances, the firewall included in a suite of software has as its main protective feature a wall that will attempt to block certain type of Internet traffic from gaining access to your computer. A computer communicates over specific streams of data called network protocols. Believe it or not, these network protocols communicate over more than 65,000 different listening ports. Consider how insecure a mega-mall would be if all the doors were left unlocked and unguarded, even the ones that customers have no business using, such as those that are to be used strictly by employees, maintenance workers, or delivery people. A computer with all of its network listening ports open and ready to accept Internet traffic is just as insecure. Consider now that most computers used in the home or for small businesses need only a small fraction of the available ports in order to communicate effectively. A software firewall can be configured to close those ports that are not commonly used. Now, since most of us don't want to go through a checklist of tens of thousands of communication ports and decide one by one which should be left open and which should be closed, most software firewalls have more generic settings. Generally, they come with a sliding scale of protection. Now, while the more restrictive settings do offer more protection, they can impact your computer's ability to communicate over the Internet. Manufacturers will have a default setting, which for most home and small-business users will likely be fine. You can always try more restrictive settings and adjust as necessary.

Lastly, there is the identity theft protection. As has been previously discussed, it's just as important to keep sensitive data from leaving your computer as it is from keeping other things from finding their way onto your computer. The identity protection part of the security suite will help you do just that. You enter in pieces of information that you want to block from being transmitted over the Internet. Examples include Social Security numbers, credit and debit card numbers, the name of your child's school, and so on. For security reasons, I recommend placing only the last four digits of your Social Security number or credit card or debit card account numbers. The software will still block the entire number from being sent, and if your computer is hacked, the bad guy will only get the truncated numbers, thus reducing your risk. When you want to allow a blocked piece of information to be sent, you'll be asked to enter in a predefined password.

Most ISPs that offer this service for their customers have partnered with a company such as McAfee or Norton and use their software. This is much cheaper for them, since they don't have to develop their own suite of protective software. After all, they're an ISP, and not an antivirus company.

The other option is when the ISP offers protective services they manage. This is usually of greater interest to small businesses than to the home computer market. Small businesses that don't have the budget to hire full-time network security experts can outsource much of the work to the ISP (assuming they provide such services). If this model works for you, it could be one of the deciding factors in choosing an ISP in the first place. Many ISPs will offer managed protective services such as firewalls, intrusion detection, antivirus, authentication services, e-mail hosting, and even vulnerability scanning and incident response. In essence, you'd be using your ISP's network, trusting that they can keep your data secure. While more comprehensive then a suite of protective software that is free from some ISPs, this is actually a host of managed services. Obviously, these are not free, and the actual costs will vary depending on your ISP and the exact services that you choose.

HELP IS AVAILABLE

Beyond the ever-helpful ISPs, tools are available to help small businesses and even home networks to better determine the effectiveness of their security controls. You can check out how effective your firewall is by going to http://www.grc.com/default.htm and then scrolling down the pate to the "Shields up" tool. Once you've selected "Shields up," you should click on *Common Ports* to see if all your ports are in Stealth Mode. This tool identifies your computer's IP address and also does a pretty good job of explaining the findings. Aside from the site's "Shield up" utility, the site also offers a wealth of resources on other common data questions and even offers other helpful utilities. My other personal favorite is the data leak test. The best thing is that these tests are all free.

Microsoft has a free tool known as Microsoft Baseline Security Analyzer (MBSA). It is available for download from its Web site, http://www.microsoft.com. Microsoft does have different versions of their MBSA tool, as well as one specific to their Windows Vista product. Simply go to http://search.microsoft.com/Results.aspx?qsc0=0&q=MBSA&mkt=en-US&FORM=QBME1&l=1&x=12&y=11 for a listing of the different versions, as well as an explanation of each to help determine which is the most appropriate for you.

With the enormous storage capacity of today's computers, perhaps one of the biggest challenges is actually knowing what applications we actually have loaded on them. This is true for business as well as home computers. A company called Belarc has a free software inventory tool; their Web site is http://www.belarc.com, and the tool's name is Belarc Advisor. Once on the Web site, select Free Download, and then click on Belarc Advisor. This will allow you to download the Free Advisor, which will give you a good picture of what software is running on your computer. After doing so, click on the link in the report "CIS Benchmark Score." It will give you tips and suggestions on how you can better secure your computer.

One of the questions that I'm often asked is which software products are the best to help me protect my computer. There are lots of applications on the market today. Some are single purpose, such as antivirus only, or simply anti-spam, etc. Others offer what they tout as a comprehensive suite of protection. CNET (http://www.cnet.com performs reviews of many different types of software. In addition to reviewing software, CNET also reviews electronic gadgets, such as laptops, cell phones, digital cameras, MP3 players, and more. The site can be a wealth of good information.

A free Internet tool called "Spybot" will search your computer and look for known spyware. Once the tool has identified the spyware, you are given the option to remove them. Spybot also has a capability called "immunize." It will help your computer better defend itself against spyware. There's another free software product called CCleaner, the web site is http://www.ccleaner.com. A system optimization and privacy tool, CCleaner will remove unused files from your computer, which not only frees up hard drive space, but also can make your system run faster. The CCleaner Web site also has links to other recommended freeware products including Recuva, a free file recovery tool, and Defraggler, which will clean up disk fragmentation; both products are located at http://www.recuva.com. A fragmented hard drive will cause a computer to run slower. Consider a fragmented computer hard drive to be akin to a large closet with clothes scattered everywhere. The task of finding the particular pants, shirt, necktie, vest, and coat needed to assemble a suit can be a difficult task, requiring you to search every inch of the closet. Consider how the same task of finding the various parts of a suit would be easier in a well-organized closet. Disk fragmentation on a computer has similar effects. The files that happen to be located in a random or fragmented nature on the computer's hard drive make the task of retrieval much more difficult.

ANTIVIRUS SOFTWARE: KEEP IT CURRENT

No matter what antivirus product you ultimately purchase, the most important thing to do is to keep it current. Antivirus programs are reactive in nature; they react to known virus programs. As new viruses are written, antivirus programs need to be updated so they will be able to recognize and block the new threats. Antivirus companies regularly update their antivirus definitions files to recognize new viruses as they become known. It is important to keep antivirus files up to date to get the most comprehensive level of protection. Most antivirus programs have an automatic update feature. My recommendation would be to make certain that the auto-update feature is enabled. It's simply easier to let the antivirus program keep itself up to date, rather than try to remember to check for updates on a regular basis. As often as new viruses are being written, we could find ourselves needing to check for updates daily. That's not something that I want to have to do. As important as it is to keep your computer's antivirus up to date, it is equally important to have it running. The term used is "real-time" protection. This will have the effect of having the anti-virus programming running all the time in the background so your computer is protected from viruses.

OPERATING SYSTEM FIXES AND UPDATES

In addition to what can be considered after-market protective software such as antivirus and antispam applications, your computer's operating system and Windows office programs (Word, Excel, Outlook) need to be kept current as well. The term used is called patching. Some patches are designed to plug security holes, while others are more performance-related. As with the antivirus definition files, the best way to keep these applications current on their patches is to have the computer do it automatically. To define the patching options in Microsoft Windows XP, do the following:

- Click the Start button and then select Control Panel
- On the Control Panel, select Automatic Updates
- On the Automatic Updates panel, select the option to "Automatically check for update daily."

The automatic patching update feature is enabled by default in the Windows Vista operating system. My recommendation would be to leave it enabled. You can however define patching options in Windows Vista by doing the following:

- Click the Start button and then select Control Panel
- On the Control Panel, under the Security category, select Check for Updates
- On the Windows Update panel, select the Change Settings option
- Select the option to automatically install updates daily.

HARDWARE FIREWALLS

It is not uncommon for large companies to have a large number of firewalls forming a protective perimeter around their entire computer network. For smaller networks, one firewall per physical location will likely be fine. As with protective software products, there are lots of hardware firewalls designed for small networks. Web sites such as http://www.networkworld.com and http://www.firewallguide.com review many different types of firewalls designed for both small businesses and home networks. Many of these are multifunction firewalls. Many can accommodate a number of computers cabled directly into them, as well as a larger number of wireless computer clients. Some also act as a printer server, allowing you to connect your printer to the firewall, so it can be shared by all computers that are on the same network. Some popular brands of firewalls include Barracuda, NetGear, and Linksys. Now, these and other companies sell various models of firewalls, so do your research to determine which one is best for your needs.

Most of these products will work just fine to protect small networks, whether they're located at your place of business or in your home. Some are strictly "wired," requiring a network capable of connecting it to your computer. They also vary in terms of capacity—simply put, the number of computers that can be plugged into them. Others are a combination of "wired" and "wireless." Make sure you get the model that meets your specific individual needs.

To confuse matters, many firewalls will refer to themselves as "routers," or, in the era of high-speed Internet connectivity, "broadband routers." As the name would lend one to believe, a router does, in fact, route traffic. In large networks, routers direct traffic from one segment of the network to the next, generally from router to router, for ultimate delivery to its destination. For small networks, these combination broadband routers/firewalls allow traffic to go from one computer to the other, as well as to other devices such as printers and scanners, and, yes, on to the Internet. They will not only route traffic, but the firewall component will help protect your systems as well.

LOW-TECH HACKING

A common misconception is that hacking always involved techno-computer geeks running sophisticated attacks in order to steal information. Sometimes, stealing your information isn't any more ingenious than peering over your shoulder and seeing what's displayed on your laptop monitor. It's actually called "shoulder surfing." Fortunately, there are simple things you can do to protect yourself against somebody who is shoulder surfing and trying to read what's displayed on your laptop. First of all, be aware of your surroundings. If you're working in a crowded public place, be aware of the risk of shoulder surfers. Most often, they are not actively trying to steal your data; it's more likely that they are just nosy. There are privacy filters that can be installed over your laptop monitor. They black out the screen for people trying to see what you're doing at an angle, while allowing you to work looking at it straight on. They also have an added antiglare feature, which is nice if you like to work outside. These types of privacy screens work great to hide your data from people sitting next to you on an airplane flight, or beside you in a Internet café. It's still important to be aware of your surroundings, since privacy screens won't obscure your data from the shoulder surfer who is behind you and not off at an angle.

AVOID DATA LOSS

The risks to data are not limited to the illicit acts of hackers trying to steal your information. Many computer viruses are specifically designed to cause data loss. A sudden loss of electrical power can cause data loss. I can remember my wife (then my fiancée) and I compiling the guest list for our upcoming wedding when her dog, a cute little beagle named Carly Simon, accidentally stepped on the power strip, turning off both the word-processing program and the computer. To this day I wonder who didn't get invited to our wedding as a result of that incident. Save your work often so that a sudden glitch, or loss of power, will only cause a data loss up to the last time you saved your work.

The risk to a computer goes beyond the sudden and unexpected loss of electrical power. Like any electronic device with moving parts, a computer can have mechanical malfunctions. The fastest-moving component on a computer is the hard drive, spinning at speeds of up to 10,000 revolutions per minute. If a hard drive fails, and they do fail, the data stored on it in most cases will be lost. This can include your family photos, your tax returns, your customer list, the homework assignment you've been working on for months, or any other kind of high-value information that you would hate to lose. One of the best ways to protect your data from being lost in the event of a hard drive failure is to back it up. There are a number of ways to do this. Thumb drives, writeable CDs, even external hard drives can all be used to make backup copies of your sensitive data. There are also tape drives designed for the needs of smaller networks. DAT drives, as they are called, actually use what look like small cassette tapes. While designed for small businesses, most modern DAT tapes have impressively large capacity.

Backing up your sensitive data on any of the removable media storage devices that I've mentioned will work just fine. Bear in mind that if you store the tape or thumb drive or writable CD in the same location as your computer, and the building is lost due to a fire or other event, your backup will be lost as well. To make certain that the data you've backed up does not suffer the same fate as your computers, don't keep them both in the same physical location. This can be as simple as having your computers at work, and the backup media in your home. For security purposes, you may want to consider storing your backup media in a bank's safe deposit box.

It is not common to back up the entire contents of your computer's hard drive. The reason is that it's assumed that you already have copies of the operating system, Microsoft Office, and any other programs that you've loaded on your computer. In essence, you already have a backup copy and don't need to make other ones. The various versions of the Windows operating system actually come with their own backup software. The one real benefit of backing up everything on your computer, at least once, with the

Windows software is that it will also create an emergency restore disk, which can be used to help restore your system in the event of a major failure. I often wonder how many end users would feel comfortable trying to rebuild their computer after a major system failure. While that is certainly an option, in most cases, what you really want to make sure you back up is data that is important to you, whether it be e-mails, spreadsheets, documents, presentations, photos, whatever. In order to access the Windows backup software, perform the following steps.

- Right click on the My Computer icon, and click on Explore
- Right click on the C drive icon
- Left click on Properties
- Left click on the Tools tab
- Left click on the Backup Now button

You will note that the backup software natively doesn't include backing up data that you have on removable media, such as thumb drives or CDs. However, there is a "Wizard" that will help you add that feature if desired. The backup software will also allow you to choose from a handful of default settings. The settings are:

- My Documents and Settings
  - Includes the My Documents folder, plus Favorites, desktops, and cookies.
- Everyone's Documents and Settings
  - Includes every user's My Documents folder, plus their Favorites, desktops, and cookies.
- All information on this computer
  - Includes all the data on the computer, and creates a system recovery disk that can be used to restore Windows in the case of a major failure.
- Let me choose what to back up

If you're going to go through the effort to back up your data, make sure it's time well spent. Do not place the data that you are trying to protect on the same computer. In essence, you would be creating a second copy on the same system, and most likely the same hard drive. If something were to happen to the computer or its hard drive, both the original copy and the backup version of your data would very likely be lost. In essence, the only thing you would be doing is using up twice the hard drive by storing two copies of the data.

Back up the data to a removable device such as a writeable CD or a thumb drive.

Beyond using the backup software that comes with Windows, some companies will back up your data over the Internet for a fee. Companies such as Carbonite, DataDepositBox, and AmeriVault offer online backup services of your computer files. Since these and other online companies that offer online backup services store your data remotely, a single event that caused the loss of your computer will not affect the data stored at their location. They are also relatively inexpensive. As of this writing, the quoted online price for this type of over-the-Internet remote data backup costs around $50 per year. DataDepositBox charges based on the amount of data you actually send them, while many others charge a flat rate. Either way, they are all relatively inexpensive. These companies all state that they use encryption as a way to tout the fact that the privacy of their customer's data is protected. These types of services are a good way to back up your data at a remote location. Of course, if they are hacked, your data *may* be exposed as well.

Perhaps a bigger risk than that of a hacker is if the company suffers a loss of their computers. If the computer that they are using to store your data is lost in a fire or other event such as a hurricane or an earthquake, your backup data could be lost as well. Some companies will back up your data in multiple locations, thus offering a level of protection if they were to lose a facility as a result of a natural disaster. Ask before your sign up for an over-the-Internet backup solution. Whether or not they store your data in multiple locations, also consider the fate of your data if the company that you use for data storage goes out of business. If a data loss would imperil the very survival of your business, don't put all your eggs in one basket. Consider using a twofold backup strategy. This could include backing up your data on some kind of removable media as well as using an over-the-Internet backup service. This way, a total loss of data would require the loss of your computer, your removable media, and a loss of your on-line backup service provider. The odds of all those events happening at the same time are very remote, thus offering your critical data a pretty good chance of surviving any single event.

PROTECTING VALUABLE DATA ON PAPER

As important as it is to protect your sensitive data that is in electronic form, it's also important to protect valuable paper documents as well. Documents such as marriage licenses, birth certificates, wills, passports, and more are not only very valuable, but also can be very difficult to replace.

Document	How to Safeguard It
Passport or visa	Keep the original in an in-house fire-proof safe or a bank safe deposit box. Keep a photo copy in a carry-on bag when traveling in a foreign country.
Birth certificate, death certificate, marriage license, Social Security Card	In-house fireproof safe or a bank safe deposit box.
Medical records, living will, last will and testament	In-house fireproof safe or a bank safe deposit box.
Family heirlooms, such as birth announcements, graduation announcements, personal cards/letters, family photos, etc.	In-house fireproof safe—if multiple copies exist, consider storage at a separate location such as at the home of a trusted friend or family member.
Bank account statements, insurance documents, previous year's tax returns (past seven years)	Locked file cabinet in your home.
Stock certificates, bonds, and other negotiable documents such as bearer bonds	In-house fireproof safe or a bank safe deposit box.
Credit and debit cards when not being carried on your person	In an in-house locked cabinet or safe.

Perhaps even more challenging than protecting data that we all have on our workstations and laptops is keeping track of the information that we have stored on our PDAs. Whether we're talking about Blackberries, Apple iPods, or any other type of PDA, our data is getting ever more mobile with every passing year. With greater mobility comes increased challenges on protecting the data that we're carrying with us.

Chapter 8

PROTECT YOUR CELL PHONES AND PDAs

Even at my tender young age, somewhere in my 40s, I can remember a world without cell phones. Long before the invention of the cell phone, there was its predecessor, the pager. When they first came into being generally, only doctors carried pagers. Also known as a beeper, the pager was invented by Multitone Electronics back in 1956 at St. Thomas' Hospital in London. It was a way to alert doctors of emergencies. Then all of a sudden, pagers suddenly became "cool," and yuppies everywhere carried one—two, if you wanted to let everybody know that you were really important.

Flash forward to the present day, and the old-style pager has gone the way of the typewriter and the eight-track tape player. Today, almost everybody has a cell phone. In fact today many adults would probably feel lost if they accidently left the house without their trusty cell phone. How did our parents and grandparents ever get along without them? I've even seen young teens on skateboards and bicycles talking on cell phones.

The first generation of cell phones had their challenges. If you remember, the old-style cell phones were also called bricks. This is due to the fact that they were the approximate size and weight of a masonry brick. What could be considered a close relative to the cell phone was the car phone. When the first car phone came out, they drew so much power from a car battery that the joke at the time was that you would place two phone calls from a car phone. The first call could be to whomever you wanted, and the second call would then be for a tow truck, because your car battery was dead. However, the need to be able to make phone calls while on the go was there.

Today's cell phones, of course, are small and sleek, with batteries that last for days on a single charge. In our world, it is considered blasé to have a cell phone that is just a cell phone. Single-function cell phones are actually in the minority, as the multifunction devices of today are far more popular. Many are Internet-aware devices capable of texting, sending and receiving e-mails, playing games, and keeping your calendar, and some come with pretty fair digital cameras. Most cell phones also come complete with an entire selection of ringtones to choose from, thus enabling users to personalize their cell phone experience even more. If that is not enough, you can also go online to download a ringtone to fit your liking. Most cell phone manufactures have ringtones that their customers can download, and some Web sites sell ringtones. Hedwig's theme is popular among the Harry Potter aficionados that I know. You can also download wallpaper images for your cell phone. Pictures of just about any theme, whether it is nature, sports, or anything else—the list goes on and on—are available. If you'd like, many will even allow you to use a favorite family photo as a wallpaper image.

CELL PHONE RECEPTION

Poor cell phone reception was also a big challenge when they first made their way onto the scene. The problem of poor reception was actually twofold. First, when cell phones first appeared in the marketplace, not that many cell phone towers were deployed yet. To make matters worse, the range of the older cell phones was also very limited. While most major cities generally have pretty good cell phone coverage, more remote places can still be hit or miss. When making a cell phone purchase, it's important to take into account where you will be using your phone. If you live in a remote area, or regularly go hiking and camping, and want good coverage, make sure to ask those questions before your buy. A basic level of cell phone service is also generally limited to within the United States only. If you want your cell phone to work in Mexico, Canada, and overseas, you will need to get a service plan that includes international coverage. Prices on making international calls can vary greatly. Don't let your first cell phone bill cause you sticker shock. Before your start dialing, ask your service provider about pricing plans that fit how you use your cell phone, including international plans as appropriate.

INTERNET-BASED PHONE SERVICE

In what can be considered a high-tech marriage made in heaven, there are now companies that allow you to utilize the Internet in order to make your phone calls. Voice over Internet Protocol (VoIP) is quickly becoming a popular alternative to traditional telephone service. VoIP works with traditional telephones and requires an adapter as well as Internet access. High-speed Internet access such as DSL or cable will result in better telephone reception than an old-style modem connection. VoIP depends on having access to the Internet; if your Internet access is down, your VoIP will not work. Since many people have cell phones anyway, they can always act as a backup telephone service.

VoIP service plans are usually cheaper than old-style phone service plans for homes and businesses that have high call volumes, and are certainly cheaper if you make a lot of international calls. One of the major differences is that you can take your VoIP telephone service with you. You can take your VoIP adapter with you, and as long as your destination has both a telephone and Internet access, you'll be able to use your VoIP service. Consider the advantage of being able to use your local telephone number while traveling around the country or even internationally. Those placing calls to you will certainly appreciate not having to pay international long-distance charges. Plans and restrictions do vary from one company to another, so make sure that you get the features that best fit your particular needs.

RISKS ASSOCIATED WITH INTERNET PHONES

VoIP telephone calls are transmitted over the Internet. As with any data sent over the Internet, there are privacy and data security risks that are not an issue with the "old-style" telephone service. VoIP telephone services are also subject to computer viruses and worms. Always looking for a way to clog up the works, spammers have created a new type of spam known as Spam over Internet Telephony (SPIT). This usually takes the form as having a huge number of voice mail messages left in your inbox. It's important to keep in mind that while these exploits do exist, there are benefits to using VoIP telephones. An obvious one is that VoIP service is usually less expensive than more traditional telephone service. The cost savings can be significant if you make a large amount of long distance calls.

Like more traditional telephone lines, your home's Internet connection can go down from time to time. You can lose Internet connectivity for a number of reasons. Your ISP can be experiencing an outage, your cable modem or DSL modem can fail, etc. If you don't want to risk being without phone service, it's important to have a backup plan. For many people, that can be as simple as having a cell phone. If your primary phone service is down, whether it's VoIP or traditional, you can always use your cell phone.

DISTRACTED DRIVING, A.K.A. THE CELL PHONE–ASSISTED CAR CRASH

Most of us are guilty from time to time of distracted driving—talking on a cell phone when we ought to be giving our full attention to being a good defensive driver. Would you want the bus driver being distracted by a cell phone as he is driving 40 children, including yours, to school? The automobile industry is starting to come out with cell phone controls built right into the steering wheel. This way you can still place your cell phone call, but you do not have to dial the number on your cell phone, thus keeping both hands on the steering wheel. The conversation will come over the car radio, which is more convenient than contorting yourself to be able to listen to your cell phone while driving. On a personal note, since I drive, too: Please, no text messaging while driving.

Of course, long before cell phones came into our lives, people found other ways to distract themselves while behind the wheel. Whether it's men shaving, ladies putting on makeup, or—my personal favorite—having the street map opened up over the steering wheel and reading it trying to find where the next turn is, distracted driving is as old as the invention of the horseless buggy itself. Cell phones did not create the issue of distracted driving; they just gave us another way to do it. Another way to talk on the cell phone while driving, while minimizing the disruptive influence, is to use a hands-free wireless headset.

BLUETOOTH

The short-range wireless technology that allows your cell phone to be controlled by buttons on the steering wheel or to communicate with a wireless headset that's attached to your ear is called Bluetooth. While commonly used with cell phones, Bluetooth technology is also what makes wireless keyboards, wireless mice, and even wireless printers possible. Perhaps a more hip example would be the wireless controllers for the Nintendo Wii.

The actual idea for the cell phone came from the 1960s science fiction television series *Star Trek*. (Martin Cooper, the man who invented the cell phone, really did get his inspiration from the inventive minds of that 1960s science fiction series.) The science fiction of the handheld wireless communicator back then is today's science fact. In fact, the earpieces of today remind me a little of what Lieutenant Uhura used while at her communication's post on the bridge of the Starship Enterprise. So, to a certain extent, we owe a degree of thanks to the creative genius of the late Gene Roddenberry, the creator of *Star Trek*, for our iPhones and Blackberries.

CELL PHONE ETIQUETTE

Many people will speak in a louder-than-normal conversational voice when talking on a cell phone. This can be somewhat annoying when it is the person next to you on the treadmill when you are trying to get in your daily exercise. If it is a quick conversation and then back to the workout, that's one thing. However, we have all seen people spend their entire time on the treadmill carrying on a very loud cell phone conversation. I'm met with mixed reactions when I ask people to either end the call or take it in the hallway so as not to disturb everybody trying to enjoy their morning routine. Think about the fact that when people listen to music in the gym, it's through a pair of headphones. Imagine what your workout experience would sound like if instead of headsets, people each had their own portable radio blaring out their favorite music.

Perhaps even worse than the gym is the fancy restaurant. When I go to a family restaurant with my kids, I expect a certain level of noise. However, when my wife and I treat ourselves to a "date" and go out to a fancy restaurant, the last thing I want is somebody carrying on a loud cell phone conversation and thus ruining the ambiance. Perhaps the worst case is when a loud cell phone ringer goes off, and then the person carries on a long, distracting conversation right in the middle of a movie, a church service, or even at a wedding or a funeral. That is a definite lack of decorum. The main reason why you are not allowed to use a cell phone while flying on airplanes is not that it will interfere with the pilot's ability to do his job; it is that the industry didn't want its customers trapped in a flying metal tube to be forced to listen to 100 competing cell phone conversations for the entire duration of the flight. I am also always amazed that people will talk about very personal things on their cell phones in very crowded public places. They are often the same people who will glare at you if they think you are listening in on their private conversation. The truth is that they're being so loud, that everybody within a pretty wide radius is hearing their conversation as well.

Casual friends and coworkers will often use the term "TMI," which stands for "too much information," when somebody freely shares a piece of rather personal information—information that they'd just as soon had not have been made privy to. The same can hold true when talking about very personal topics on a cell phone in a crowded public place. Perhaps what is even more offensive is when people use foul language during cell phone conversations in crowded places. I'd just as soon my young children not hear the "f" word or other swear words when we are in the local mall, or trying to go grocery shopping. I definitely don't want my young kids to hear how you "got lucky last night," either. I'm happy for you, but please keep it to yourself.

NUMBER PAD LOCKS

Many models of cell phones come with the ability to lock their number pads. If you are carrying your cell phone in a carrier or your purse, you don't want it to accidentally call somebody. Perhaps even more embarrassing is having your young child playing with your cell phone and accidentally calling your boss at work. While my then-three-year-old son never did call my manager, he did have a very pleasant conversation with one of my coworkers. She's a parent herself and thought the entire situation was rather amusing. I started locking the number pad on my cell phone after that incident, however.

Aside from stopping the curious child, locking the number pad on your cell phone will also help protect it if it's ever lost or stolen. Thieves would like nothing more than to run up hundreds of dollars of long-distance phone charges on your stolen cell phone. The charges can get very expensive quickly if they start calling those 900-number adult phone sex sites. Locking the number pad on your cell phone will also help protect the names and phone numbers of the people that you have stored on your address book. So, locking the number pad of your cell phone will help protect yourself as well as your contacts.

If your cell phone is ever lost or stolen, call your service provider right away to report it. You can get their number off of your monthly statement, or off of the service contract. In most cases, you can also get their contact information right from their Web site. Most companies will be able to deactivate your cell phone remotely so that nobody can use it. They will also be happy to send you another cell phone as well. Of course, depending on the exact model of cell phone that you had, you may find yourself having to purchase the replacement phone.

PASSWORD PROTECT YOUR PERSONAL DIGITAL ASSISTANT (PDA)

Unlocking the number pad on a cell phone generally requires the user to enter in a password. Your personal digital assistant (PDA) can often also be password protected as well. This will not only help prevent people from making telephone calls on your PDA, but it can also help protect any sensitive data that you might have stored on it. PDAs can store much more than just phone lists. Major manufacturers of PDAs, such as Blackberry and the Apple iPhones, also offer encryption as a way to further protect the data that you store on them. As encryption is designed to protect data from unauthorized users, providing for the protection of your password becomes even more important. If you tape your password to the back of your PDA, the person who just stole it can just type it in and bypass the encryption. I return again to the major theme of my book: Data security is more of a human issue than a technical one.

BLUESNARFING AND BLUEJACKING

What would be the impact if your PDA was lost or stolen? Would it mean that your entire phone list would be gone? Would it expose those on your phone list, including family, friends, coworkers, and customers, to unsolicited calls from the stranger who now has your PDA? There are also hackers out there that will try to steal the data right off your PDA. As previously discussed, PDAs use the Bluetooth wireless data transmission technology. Well, there are hacking risks that specifically target Bluetooth: Bluesnarfing and Bluejacking.

Bluejacking is the practice of sending unsolicited messages to Bluetooth-enabled devices. It's like getting junk mail or unsolicited e-mails. There is actually a Web site dedicated to Bluejacking, http://www.BlueJackQ.com. It provides Bluejacking software as well as tips and tricks. A kind of "how to" Web site for hacking actually follows an unfortunate trend in the hacker universe. Many Web sites offer free and often very easy-to-use hacking tools. This makes it possible for people with even minimal levels of technical computer knowledge to carry out hacking attacks with relative ease. It has become such an epidemic that low-skilled hackers using these preconfigured tools are now referred to as "script kiddies." I suppose the high-skilled hackers wanted a term to denote the more novice-level members of the hacking community.

Another hacker attack that specifically targets Bluetooth-enabled cell phones and PDAs is known as Bluesnarfing. It is actually a more serious threat than Bluejacking, as Bluesnarfing entails a hacker gaining unauthorized access to your PDA to see data that you have stored on it. Examples include such things as your contact list, business calendar, e-mails, text messages, and any other data that you might have stored on your cell phone or PDA.

There are steps you can take to protect the data on your cell phone and PDA from both of these attacks. Set your Bluetooth-enabled device to "undiscoverable" as a way to combat both Bluesnarfing and Bluejacking. Download the latest version of the Bluetooth software appropriate for your PDA. Similar to installing security patches for your computer, ensuring you have the latest version of Bluetooth on your PDA will also help block these attacks. Utilizing a combination of passwords, encryption, and proper system configuration, it is possible to greatly reduce the risks to our cell phones and PDAs. Remember, in most cases, hackers are looking for the easy target and will generally bypass those who have placed security hurdles in their way.

MP3 PLAYERS

It is not uncommon for people to want to listen to their favorite music while at work. With an MP3 player and a set of headphones, you can listen to your favorite music for hours while working the day away. Many models of MP3 players actually recharge themselves off of a computer battery. You plug them into your computer, using the USB port to recharge them. I want to provide a word of caution here. While designed to store music files, an MP3 player is also a portable mass-storage device. It will store any type of data that is written to it. If you don't want to accept the risk of your company's sensitive data being copied to an MP3 player, don't allow them to be connected to your work computers. Many portable radios with CD players are also MP3 compatible. Most also have input jacks for headphones. You employees can still listen to their favorite songs over their headsets without attaching an external mass-storage device to a company computer.

It is important to understand that we are all human, and as such, we are susceptible to mental lapses from time to time. Senior moments or no, they happen to the best of us. How many of us can honestly say that we've never misplaced our car keys? In the digital age that we live in, losing a laptop can cause problems that go well beyond the loss of the actual hardware itself. So, it is best to afford the data that we have on our laptops a level of protection that goes beyond the due diligence of trying not to misplace it.

Chapter 9

AVOID THEFT AND LOSS OF HARDWARE

O ne of the most common sources of data loss is the loss of a device that contains your personal or business information. Have you ever lost your wallet, your purse, your cell phone, your PDA, or even your laptop? If you haven't, odds are that you know somebody who has. Now, industries that are heavily regulated, such as banks, have a vested interest in ensuring that any sensitive data on these types of devices are well protected so they can not easily be "hacked" if the device itself is lost or stolen. With that said, protecting data goes beyond banks and credit card companies. A salesperson in a small business wants to safeguard her customer list. An owner of a restaurant wants to protect recipes that he has developed over the years and that draw in big crowds night after night. It could be as simple as wanting to avoid that creepy feeling of having a total stranger read the e-mails on the laptop that you've just lost or had stolen. Simply put, sensitive information is data that is important to you. It's information that you wouldn't want to fall in the hands of a stranger.

SENSITIVE DATA EQUATES TO GREATER RISK

Depending on the nature of the data that you have stored on your electronic devices, losing them can involve exposing your employees, your customers, and even your business to a substantial amount of risk. Consider the ramifications of losing a device that had information on it, such as customer credit card information, employee health information, or even personnel files, including the Social Security numbers of all your employees. You could very likely face the ire (or legal actions) of your customers or your employees if losing data on them leads to identity theft. If the lost data included information about you and your family, you may very well be facing the ire of your loved ones.

Consider the possible career ramifications of losing data like salary information about your manager. If it's your job at work to ensure that your company's electronic data is secure, a data breach could very well be a career-limiting event for you. It's not uncommon for many people to hold the "security guy" responsible if they are victimized by a hacker. While this may be an rather unfair level to be held to, in many cases, if you're the security guy, it's your reality. This is particularly true if your responsibilities far outstretch your authority—a phenomenon not unheard of in the data security field. It's also very hard to anybody to effectively protect electronic data if the end users themselves are engaging in unsafe practices. Remember, data security is more of a human issue than a technical one. It is for that very reason that I am a strong advocate of utilizing security controls that are not dependent on human interaction for their effectiveness. An example would be antivirus software that is both always on and automatically updates itself. Along those same lines, there are technologies that you can deploy on laptops to help keep the data safe, even if the owner doesn't necessarily embrace safe data security practices.

PROTECTING DATA ON LAPTOPS

We humans all too often turn out to be the greatest data security risk we have. That means that in business, in almost every instance, your greatest security risk—or, with proper awareness, your greatest security asset—are your employees. In the case of a home-based business, that could be you and your family. If your human assets have a casual attitude towards data security, even the most fancy gadget is going to be somewhat diminished in its quest to keep your electronic data secure. That said, since we are all human and do have mental lapses now and then, there are things we can do to help protect us from ourselves.

A part of my job entails travel. Whether it's meetings with senior management or speaking at security seminars, my laptop and I have seen a fair amount of this great country of ours. There are some simple things that I do to limit the risks of my losing my laptop. When I leave my house to go to the airport, for example, I go directly there. I don't make any stops at convenience stores, or anyplace that would require that I leave my car. I hear all too often how laptops are stolen from unattended vehicles, whether they're left visible on the front seat or even locked in the trunk. I have even seen laptops, purses, and other valuables left in convertibles that had their tops down. By going directly (non-stop) from my house to the airport, I've just eliminated the risk to my laptop of having it stolen right out of my unattended car.

I've also trained myself to keep a close eye on my laptop when going through airport security. Depending on how busy the airport is on a given day, the security checkpoint can be a very congested and distracting area.

Also bear in mind that when going through a security checkpoint in a U.S. airport, you'll be required to remove your laptop from its carrying case. I place something of mine in front of my laptop as well as behind it. This strategy helps remove any doubt that the particular laptop is, in fact, mine. Since laptops can tend to look alike, especially the same model and manufacturer, consider placing a sticker on yours to help personalize it and thus remove any doubt of ownership. It doesn't necessarily have to be your name and address; a Disneyland sticker from your last family vacation would do just fine. What you don't want to place on your laptop is a post-it note that contains your username and password. While this may seem obvious. I've seen it done in companies that bragged about their "high security." Like I said, data security is a human issue more so than a technical one.

Unattended Laptops

Here in the twenty-first century, many of us work on our laptops in airport terminals, coffee houses, and Internet cafés just about anywhere. I have even worked on parts of this book in any number of airport terminals around the country, and while taking an Amtrak train from Washington, DC, to New York. While working in these public areas, consider the risk of leaving your laptop unattended for even a couple of minutes. We all need to go to the bathroom from time to time, after all. When my wife and I go out to dinner, if she needs to excuse herself, I am often reminded to keep an eye on her purse. Obviously, a woman's purse contains valuables such as cash, credit/debit cards, a driver's license, and any number of other items. Having your purse stolen would first mean the loss of any valuables. Next, you'd have to call your credit card companies to cancel all your cards. Losing your driver's license would require that you contact your local motor vehicle office to order a new one. The list goes on and on, but you get the point. Losing your laptop can have similar, and even bigger, ramifications.

By now, some of you are thinking that I take my laptop into bathroom stalls with me. Well, you know what? You are correct. If my laptop is with me when I am in a public place, it's with me at all times; that includes any required visits to the men's room. Now, if I'm traveling with my wife or a trusted coworker, I ask that person to keep an eye on my laptop for me. You might also consider investing in a cable lock for your laptop. Akin to locks used to protect bicycles when we leave them attached to parking stands or light posts, there are cable locks designed specifically for laptop computers. Most, if not all, laptop models are designed to accommodate these types of cable locks. So, if you're working alone in that coffee house, consider tethering your laptop to the table. It will offer your laptop a degree of security when you need to step away for a couple of minutes. If you think I'm sounding somewhat extreme now, consider this as being similar to leaving an unattended purse. Bear in mind that most thieves are opportunistic and will look for the easy snatch-and-run of the unattended and unprotected laptop. It is, of course, possible to cut through a set of cable locks using a pair of bolt cutters. However, it would be considered somewhat suspicious for somebody to be sitting at the corner Starbucks carrying a set of bolt cutters with them. Then again, if you see a suspicious person with a set of bolt cutters, take your laptop to the bathroom with you. You could be saving your laptop as well as your cable lock.

HOTEL ROOMS

If you're traveling with your laptop and staying in a hotel room, there are challenges in protecting it. Most hotels don't have in-room safes. Of those that do, the safes may only be large enough to accommodate smaller items such as passports, credit cards, jewelry, and cash. This is because hotels started installing in-room safes long before the advent of the laptop. When deciding on what hotel to stay at, consider asking if they have in-room safes, and whether or not they are large enough to accommodate a laptop. In lieu of in-room safes, some hotels will have safe deposit boxes that are available for customers to use while staying there. While they are not in the room, they also offer a degree of physical protection for your laptop as well as other valuables. Absent those two options—you guessed it—I'm carrying my laptop with me at all times. I also perform a sweep of the entire hotel room before I leave to check out. While something as large as a laptop might be hard to forget, I don't want to lose my cell phone, my watch, or my thumb drive, either. If your hotel has an in-room safe, make sure it's open and empty before you leave to check out. You don't want to lose your valuables by accidently leaving them in the very safe that the hotel provided for you in order to protect them.

SMALL + PORTABLE = EASIER TO LOSE

The hard truth is that as devices get smaller and smaller, they also become easier to lose. Consider the fact that back in the 1980s and 1990s, it wasn't common practice for people to be walking around carrying floppy disks. Even if we did lose one, their storage capacity was only 1.4 megabytes. It was also less likely that we would forget our 1980s-era cell phone. It was somewhat harder to accidently misplace a bulky and heavy brick phone than the cell phones of today, some of which are only slightly larger than a credit card. Along the lines of easy-to-lose devices, today we have thumb drives that can hold thousands of times more data than the old floppy disks could. For most small and home-based businesses, you can store information on every customer, every gadget, every marketable idea that you have on a device that's roughly the size of a cigarette lighter. If the thumb drive were to fall out of your pocket or purse, or be left behind in that hotel room, whoever found it would likely have easy access to any and all data that you've placed on it. Some models of thumb drives are designed to hook onto a key ring. The thought here, of course, is that we're less likely to misplace our car keys that also have our thumb drive on it, than our thumb drive all by itself. Other steps can also be taken to help protect sensitive data on laptops, thumb drives, and other removable media in case they are lost or stolen.

ENCRYPTION

A number of companies sell software that will encrypt the entire hard drive of a laptop. Companies such as PointSec, PGP, and McAfee Endpoint Encryption offer such solutions. I like solutions that encrypt the entire hard drive, as it doesn't require an end user to try to decide which data is and is not sensitive enough to encrypt. Hard-drive encryption will protect the data on a laptop if it is lost or stolen. You would then limit your liability to the cost of replacing the actual laptop itself and any downtime in doing so. That could be much more cost effective than losing every piece of sensitive data, including any company "secrets" that were stored on what is now that lost or stolen laptop. I only half-jokingly said earlier not to have your username and password taped to your laptop, because I have seen it done all too often. By doing so, and thus providing the hacker with your username and password, you're giving them all that they need to bypass the hard-drive encryption.

It is important to bear in mind that hard-drive encryption is not the same as file-level encryption. Hard-drive encryption is designed only to protect data from somebody who has just powered the system on. Before fully booting up, you'll be challenged to enter in a username and password in order to proceed past the hard-drive encryption software. However, once the laptop is powered on and you log into the operating system, hard-drive encryption won't protect your individual data files. If an unauthorized person (hacker) gets access to your computer after you've passed the hard-drive encryption username and password challenge they will be able to read any data that's on your laptop in unencrypted form, also referred to as "clear text." Specific file-level encryption is required to protect individual files that are stored on either your laptop or workstation computer. Microsoft has encryption software, called Encrypting File System or EFS, on their newer versions of their

Windows operating system. It allows for the automatic encryption of certain files on your computer. EFS is not available on the home edition version of Windows XP. While there are companies that sell encryption software for us with Windows XP home edition, my suggestion would be to purchase the professional edition of Windows XP for your home computer if you require file-level encryption.

Removable Media Encryption

Whether it's a thumb drive, or a CD to which you've copied data with your laptop's CD burner, you can place sensitive data on removable media as well. The same solutions that will encrypt your laptop's entire hard drive will also encrypt the data that's on these types of removable devices. The term is actually called removable media encryption (RME). Since not every hard-drive encryption solution also has RME, if that's a must-have for you, ask before you decide to buy. RME can be configured in a number of different ways. It can encrypt by default, requiring users to consciously choose not to encrypt data. Conversely, it can not encrypt by default, thus requiring users to consciously choose to encrypt. You can configure it so that only other computers on your network can decrypt a device with the RME installed. This would help prevent a hacker from trying to access your data by having their own instance of the RME software on their computer. Major providers of popular PDA devices, such as Blackberry and iPhones, also offer encryption solutions. Again, if you're going to store sensitive data on these portable devices, consider protecting it with encryption.

Equipment Lists

It is important to keep an accurate list of both your hardware and your software. For hardware, you are generally talking about the manufacturer, make, model, and serial number of a particular piece of equipment. Keeping a list of what hardware your company (or your family) owns goes beyond laptops, and includes workstations, servers, printers, fax machines, monitors, PDAs, and more. Maintaining an accurate record of your hardware inventory will help you to better track your equipment expenditures. This can be very helpful at tax time to be able to substantiate such business costs. If you are documenting a loss for either tax or insurance purposes, having accurate information on it will help with those processes as well. This can also be helpful when having to replace the lost equipment. It goes without saying that if the equipment loss was actually a theft, being able to provide law enforcement with the exact make, model, and serial number of the device increases the chances that it will be returned and the thief will get prosecuted. Many thieves will try to sell stolen hardware at local pawn shops. If you're able to report the exact make, model, and serial number to the police, that might help break the case open.

As important as it is to maintain an accurate list of hardware, it's equally important to maintain an accurate list of software as well. Consider the fact that most software that we have installed on our computers had to be purchased. This includes the operating system—for most of us, some version of either Macintosh from Apple or Windows from Microsoft. Many computers also have a suite of productivity software, such as Word, Excel, Outlook, and in some cases Access and perhaps PowerPoint. That's only the beginning, of course, as the computer might also have protective software on it such as antivirus, a personal firewall, and perhaps some antispam and antispyware applications. The point here is that the loss of a piece of computing equipment such as a laptop involves more than the loss of a piece of hardware and any data that may have been stored on it; it also includes applications that have been installed on it. You don't want to compound your costs when you have to purchase a new laptop to replace the one that was just stolen by also having to purchase every piece of software that was on it. Now, in some cases that will be unavoidable. After all, when you buy a laptop, it's going to have an operating system on it. However, if you have a record of your purchase of Microsoft Office, you won't have to buy an additional copy. Ideally, you not only will have the license information, but you'll have the CD to load the data on the new laptop as well. Microsoft will even help you replace stolen software, but in order to do so, you must be able to provide a proof of purchase. There, again, is the value of keeping an accurate inventory.

MITIGATE OR ELIMINATE

There's a saying in the security field that if you can't mitigate a risk, try to eliminate it. In this context, that would mean taking steps to remove a potential risk rather than trying to put protective controls in place to mitigate it. For example, if your business deals with sensitive information and you don't want to have the risk of it floating around on employee laptops, then don't let them store data on their laptops. An even more foolproof way to eliminate the risk of losing laptops would be not to provide your employees with laptops in the first place. Workstations are far less mobile and, in most cases, are less expensive than laptops. Employees aren't very likely to ask to be able to take their bulky workstation and monitor home with them. You can eliminate a security risk and lower your cost at the same time. Another way to reduce your data security risks is to have a shared server, and to configure your employee laptops—and workstations, as the case may be—to store their data on the server rather on their local systems. At that point, if a laptop were to be lost or stolen, you won't have the added concern of losing sensitive company data as well. Most companies, even large ones, aren't very good at backing up end users' computers, such as workstations or laptops. Having data stored on a centralized system also allows you to back up the one system to protect all your employees' data. That's much cheaper, and certainly much easier to administer, than trying to ensure that every employee backs up their data.

The same "mitigate or eliminate" approach also applies to removable media. RME is a step toward mitigating the risk of having sensitive data on devices such as thumb drives and CDs. If your laptops and workstations didn't have CD burners, that would eliminate the risk of sensitive data being written to CD. CD burners are simply CD drives with the ability the write data to a CD as well as read data. CD drives that are read-only are generally less expensive than their read/write counterparts. So here we have another example of a security control that actually lowers equipment costs.

It is also possible to eliminate the risks of sensitive data being placed at risk by floating around on any number of thumb drives. You can simply have a company policy stating that data is not to be placed on thumb drives. That would actually be called an administrative control. A technical control would be to disable the ability to copy data to a thumb drive. There are a number of ways to do that. Thumb drives connect to computers by a Universal Serial Bus (USB) port. It is possible to disable the USB ports, effectively eliminating somebody's ability to use their thumb drives. This can be done by going into the computer's "device manager." In order to access your computer's device manager, perform the following steps:

- Left click on the Start button, which is located on the lower left corner of your computer display.
- Left click on the Control Panel button.
- Once in the Control Panel, left click on the System icon.
- Left click on the Hardware tab.
- Left click on the Device Manager tab; this will cause a list of your computer's hardware devices to be displayed. This list is sorted alphabetically.
- Left click on the plus sign ("+") next to the words "Universal Serial Bus controllers," and this will list the USB devices that are attached to your computer.

- Right click on each one of them and select Disable. You'll receive a popup window warning you that disabling a device will cause it to stop working, and be prompted to choose yes or no.

Choosing yes will of course disable any attached device, causing it to stop working. If you find out that you need the particular USB port to work, you can always go back in and re-enable it. No harm, no foul. I have had people express their concerns to me that by disabling their laptops' USB ports, they will disable their external mouse— which, in many cases, is also a USB device. All laptops also have an internal mouse, and some have more than one. Generally, they are in the form of either a flat surface or what looks like an eraser from a pencil. So, if you accidentally disabled your external mouse, simply go back into your Device Manager and re-enable that particular USB instance. You can still disable the other ones. Bear in mind that the same USB port that your external mouse uses can also be used by a thumb drive. It's a give-and-take, as many end users are more comfortable using an external mouse over the built-in ones. I also recommend disabling only one USB device at a time to see if you've accidently disabled a device that you do need.

A common theme throughout the book has been that in most cases, the data on the device—whether it's a laptop, a thumb drive, or your Blackberry—is more valuable than the actual piece of equipment itself. Many times, data is much more valuable than equipment. Perhaps at a personal level, no data is more sensitive than our own identity. Identity theft is a real problem in this country, so much so that companies have begun to offer products and services to help protect people from becoming victimized.

Chapter 10

COMBAT ID THEFT

If you've ever been the victim of identity them, you know firsthand that it can take years to restore both your credit and, in some cases, your good name. Thieves can use your Social Security number to apply for credit, make large purchases, and then proceed to default on them. The fallout from being a victim of identity theft can result in ruining a credit rating that you've spent a lifetime of prudent financial conduct to acquire.

PROTECT YOUR IDENTITY ONLINE

Answer this question: Do you have a file on your computer that contains all the account user names and passwords to your various online accounts? If the answer is yes, did you compound the problem by naming the account "password"? You might think this sounds funny; but, in the name of convenience, people will often make lists of their usernames and passwords. If a hacker or identity thief were to get their hands on that file, they'd have all the information they need to commit financial fraud, identity theft, or both. I have seen laptops with a user's account name and password taped to the back of it. I have also seen computer monitors with post-it notes attached to them that contained account names and passwords. Perhaps the worst thing is to keep such a detailed list so that each account name and password combination is associated with the online site that it goes to. While it is convenient for us, it is also, unfortunately, convenient for the hacker.

As I have said a number of times, data security is more of a human issue than a technology issue. On the other hand, we are all human, and trying to keep track of a bunch of different account names and passwords can be very difficult, to say the least. It can also be very inconvenient when we forget a username or password to an account that we don't access frequently. Most of us also instinctively know that it's not a real good idea to have the exact same account name and password for every online account that we have.

This would allow the would-be fraudster to access all our online accounts with relative ease.

If you're going to write down the account name and passwords that you use, I would recommend taking steps to protect that information. First, do not leave account names and passwords in plain sight. Do not tape account names and passwords to either your computer monitor or to your laptop. A certain amount of separation will provide a level of security. For example, keeping them in a locked drawer in your desk offers a degree of protection. Consider writing down a slight modification to your password that is easy for you to know, but will make the hacker's job somewhat more difficult. For example, if your password is *fox471,* consider writing down *fox582.* You would, in essence, be substituting the real numbers in your password with the next higher number. While not considered a strong defense in the sophisticated world of modern encryption, since most accounts will lock the user out after three failed attempts, this can be surprisingly effective. In fact, the substitution cipher, as it is called, was used quite effectively in Caesar's day. While the precise methodology differed, both Julius and Augustus Caesar used their own versions of a substitution cipher.

SIGNS THAT YOU'VE BEEN A VICTIM

One of the problems with identify theft is that it is not always obvious that your identity has been stolen. In fact, you might not be aware that your identity has been stolen until long after the actual theft took place. Consider the impact of receiving a notification from the Internal Revenue Service (IRS) that they are rejecting your tax return because you have undeclared sources of income that need to be accounted for. You look into it, and the IRS advises you that you have undeclared income from a job with a company you've never heard of. Somebody has used your Social Security number to gain employment. It is common practice for undocumented workers to provide prospective employers with fraudulent paperwork in order to gain employment. The odds are that they were not actually targeting you specifically, but that the nine-digit number they supplied for the I-9 Employment Eligibility Verification form just happened to be your Social Security number.

In an effort to help guard against the fraudulent use of Social Security numbers to gain employment, the federal government's Department of Homeland Security has developed a system called E-Verify. E-Verify is an Internet-based solution that employers can use to verify that the Social Security number provided does, in fact, belong to the applicant. As of this writing, E-Verify is both free and voluntary. For more information, head to http://www.dhs.gov/ximgtn/programs/gc_1185221678150.shtm.

Identity theft goes way beyond using stolen Social Security numbers to get a job. In fact, identity theft has become such an issue that companies have begun to offer services that are designed to help people protect themselves. The company FreeCreditReport.com runs catchy commercials of three young men singing about their trials and tribulations of not checking their credit scores, only to find out that they've been victims of identity theft. One has them working in a restaurant serving tourists chowder and iced tea. The other one has them driving off a car lot in an old wreck of a used subcompact car, as they are getting laughed at by two young ladies driving passed them. As they put it in the commercial, their "posse is getting laughed at." As the two commercials state, both unfortunate incidences were due to the fact that they did not check their credit scores.

Now, generally speaking, if you are conscientious about paying your bills on time, you would expect to have a pretty good credit score. The point the commercials are trying to make is that you might not know you've been a victim of identity theft until you try to apply for credit to make that high-dollar purchase or apply for a credit card. It's why companies such as FreeCreditReport.com will allow you to check your credit score for free. Under federal law, you are entitled to receive a free copy of your credit report from each of the three credit bureaus once a year. You can request your free annual credit report by going to http://www.annualcreditreport.com.

In the case of FreeCreditReport.com, upon obtaining your credit score, you are also enrolling in their credit monitoring service called Triple Advantage. They allow you to cancel the membership within seven days, or pay a nominal monthly fee while you're a member. As the name Triple Advantage would lead one to believe, they check your credit score with each of the three main credit bureaus—TransUnion, Equifax, and Experian.

The CEO of another company that provides identity theft protection, LifeLock, puts his money where his mouth is. He boasts that the credit monitoring service LifeLock offers is so good that he places his real Social Security number in commercials and in print advertisements. They also back up their service with a $1,000,000 guarantee. Other companies, such as TrueCredit and Identity Guard, also provide credit-monitoring services. Some companies that offer credit-monitoring services also provide services such as calling credit bureaus on your behalf if your wallet is ever stolen. You just call your credit-monitoring service, and they'll take it from there. Chase offers identity theft protection products as well, which they call Chase Identity Protection. Another company called NetAdvisor has capitalized on the fact that both the level of service as well as costs among the different credit monitoring companies vary. They have compiled a chart rating a many of the more popular ones. Take a look at http://www.netadvisor.com.

You may think that with a certain amount of due diligence, you don't need to pay for a credit monitoring service. You will be able to stop suspicious activity and resolve things for yourself. You can, for example, diligently check your financial statements regularly. But credit-monitoring services can almost be considered identity theft insurance. You pay a premium for the service, and you need it only if something bad happens. Credit monitoring service may be right for your particular situation, or it may not. Given the stakes, it's at least worth considering.

Perhaps one of the scariest aspects of identity theft is having the person who has stolen your identity commit a crime. There are numerous instances across the country in which the true owner of the identity has fallen under the specter of suspicion because criminal acts were committed "in their name." Imagine getting contacted by law enforcement asking you about serious felonies such as robbery or crimes against children. It is not uncommon for victims of identity theft to have to spend a great deal of time and energy in order to restore their good name as well as their credit rating.

A SIMPLE TIP TO THWART CREDIT CARD THIEVES

Just as bad are thieves who steal your credit cards and make fraudulent purchases. In some cases, they have stolen your actual credit card itself. But here's a simple way you can thwart thieves: Don't sign the back of the credit card. I don't. How exactly is the clerk supposed to know if the signature on the back of the credit card is mine or not? I suppose they could check my driver's license, as it has both my picture and my signature. That's actually never happened to me, and I also doubt most store clerks have any real training in comparing signatures.

On the back of my credit cards, I write, "Photo ID Required." Sometimes I will be asked for a picture ID, and sometimes not. I know the clerk is just going through the motions when they check the back of my credit card and give it back to me without asking for an ID. They're obviously not checking anything. However, a fair number of them, upon reading that, do ask me for a picture ID. One of my credit cards has my picture on the back. I'm still asked for a picture ID, and always direct the clerk to check the back of the card. It's quick, it's simple, and it saves me the trouble of producing a second form of identification. Most importantly, most credit card thieves would think twice before presenting a credit card with the legitimate owner's picture on it to a clerk to try to make a purchase.

WHAT TO DO IF YOU BECOME A VICTIM OF IDENTITY THEFT

If you think that you've been the victim of identity theft, you should contact the three major consumer reporting agencies:

- Equifax: 800-525-6285
- Experian: 888-397-3742
- TransUnion: 800-680-7289

In addition to the consumer reporting agencies, you should also contact the following governmental agencies:

- Social Security Administration: http://www.ssa.gov
- Department of Motor Vehicles: http://www.ftc.gov/privacy/dmv-add.htm
- Lost/stolen U.S. passport: http://travel.state.gov/passport/lost/us/us_848.html

You also want to contact your local law enforcement agency if you suspect that you've fallen victim to identity theft. This could prove particularly useful if the thief is going to commit crimes using your identity.

Things an Identity Thief Can Do When Pretending to Be You

- Apply for a job (this has become somewhat more difficult with the advent of the federal government's E-Verify system).
- Change your credit card mailing address in order to make charges on your accounts.
- Apply for a new credit card, not pay the bills, and ruin your credit rating.
- Open a checking account in your name, write bad checks, and ruin your credit rating.
- Get cash advances.
- Rent an apartment (they'll likely not pay the rent, get evicted, and again ruin your credit rating).
- Get a cell phone and run up bills in your name.
- Obtain utility services.
- Obtain a car loan or other type of loan for large-ticket items.
- Commit crimes that could affect much more than your credit rating.

I'm sure there are more things that an identity thief can do. They have all the time in the world to think of "creative" ways to use the identities that they have stolen for their own personal gain. Don't take identity theft lightly; be vigilant, and take precautions.

BUSINESSES BEWARE

If, as a consumer, you report to your credit card company that a particular purchase is in fact fraudulent, you will not be liable for the entire amount. Generally in these types of circumstances, your liability will be no more than $50. However, if you're the business that sold the fraudster the high-dollar item, you might be facing other problems altogether. The credit card company might not be willing to make good on the purchase, since it was reported as a fraud in a timely manner. Your business might very well find itself out the high-ticket item and not get paid for it, either.

If your business takes credit and debit cards, practice sound cashiering. Ask for a second form of identification, ideally one that has both a name and a photograph. If people don't have a driver's license, they can always get a state-issued photo identification card. States will issue such cards that, while not valid as a drivers' license, will act effectively as a form of identification since they also include a photo. Tourists traveling here in the United States will have a either a travel visa, a passport, or both. Passports and visas do include the owner's name, as well as a signature and photograph.

It is common for businesses to conduct checks at the time of purchase to ensure that there are sufficient funds available on the customer's credit or debit card account prior to finalizing the purchase. It's relatively easy for businesses to obtain such approval for a particular credit card purchase for most credit cards, including Visa, MasterCard, American Express, and Discover, by swiping the card in a card-reading data terminal. The terminal, which is connected to a modem line, will send the information back to the credit card company to verify a number of things. First, you will be advised if the particular credit or debit card has been reported lost or stolen. You will also be told if there are enough funds left on the card to cover the amount of the purchase. It is not uncommon for corporate credit cards to have a one-time purchase or a daily dollar limit in addition to their monthly dollar limit.

A dilemma that I've seen many companies face is this: What do you do if the credit card terminals are down and you can't check on the status of your customer's cards? Do you take the information down the old-fashioned way, by writing it out? How about using one of those clunky imprinting machines that has the sliding lever that goes back and forth to make the copies? Either way, you'll get the data, but you won't know if the card is lost, stolen, or just doesn't have enough money left on it to cover the cost of the purchase. It's a business decision. By refusing the card, you risk losing the sale and offending a customer. By accepting the sale, you risk being out both the money and the item that you have just sold them. In my mind, what is perhaps scariest about the whole issue of identity theft is the fact that many identity thieves are not targeting us as adults.

THEY'RE COMING AFTER OUR CHILDREN

The target of choice for a majority of thieves who want to steal Social Security numbers to commit identity theft and financial fraud is our children. This is due to the fact that most of our kids, particularly younger ones, have neither credit nor debit cards. Most adults have either a credit card or a debit card, and in many cases, a number of each. This means that we receive monthly statements that we can (and should) check carefully to make sure that all charges are, in fact, valid. However, identity thieves can fraudulently use children's Social Security numbers for years with only the most minimal chance that they'll be caught. Imagine how your children would feel if, upon applying for their first credit cards as young adults, they are advised that they have a bad credit history going back for years. How would they feel about being turned down for a student loan when trying to enter college? It goes without saying that most young people would be ill-equipped to know what steps to take to restore their credit rating. So, if credit monitoring is not right for you, consider getting it for your kids.

On an even more somber note, there are people out there who would cause more harm to our kids than the chaos of stealing their identities in order to commit fraud. Child predators, pedophiles, and those who would exploit children for their own ends are out there. They often use the Internet in attempts to draw kids into their webs. As parents, it's our job to safeguard our kids from such dangers.

Chapter 11

PROTECTING CHILDREN

The Internet has created access to information like no other prior invention of humankind. I look back at my own life and think how many hours I spent in college libraries conducting research for the term papers that I had to write. If only I had access to Wikipedia back in the late 1980s! Today, people can sit in front of their computers and access much more information than is contained in any library. The Internet is bringing enlightening information to people around the globe. Some regimes are so afraid to compete in the arena of ideas that they have taken steps to block access to the Internet from their people.

The Internet has allowed families that are separated by geography to write and share family photos at near real-time speeds. I can be vacationing with my wife and kids in Disneyland during the day, and sending the photos to their grandma Etta that evening. That's a huge technological leap forward from having to wait a week to get the film developed and then mail the pictures to my mother. The Internet also lets people interact with each other in new ways. Consider that the pen pal of the past is now the e-mail buddy of the present.

However, with this wondrous new invention comes a certain amount of risk. There are risks that come from people who would use the Internet for their own malicious intent that goes beyond the perils of mere hacking. Couple that with the fact that most children are too young and innocent, living in the here and now, to take appropriate precautions to help keep themselves safe and secure. Just as most 16-year-olds are not the best drivers in the world, youngsters often don't see the perils in engaging in risky behavior online, either. It is up to us as parents to protect our children. The balancing act is giving them the information that they need to be safe, while at the same time not destroying their innocence.

THE VALUE OF BEING CAMERA SHY

As with any piece of technology, if the Internet is used improperly, bad things can happen. I'm talking as a parent now. Young girls, teens, and in some cases even preteens are far too often sharing photos of themselves that are very suggestive. Whether they are sending a half-naked picture of themselves to a boyfriend, or just girls "playing around," what many would consider inappropriate pictures—if not sexually explicit—of teenage girls often find their way onto social networking sites or are sent to far too many people in e-mails. That sexy picture your daughter only meant to be e-mailed to her boyfriend is now the talk of her entire high school. Even if the boyfriend has enough self-restraint not to e-mail his girlfriend's sexy picture to his buddies, what happens after the breakup, when Mister Wonderful all of a sudden isn't so wonderful anymore?

While this is not a book on family values, I do believe that as parents, we need to have frank discussions with our children in order to protect them from the embarrassment of having sexually revealing/suggestive pictures of themselves finding their way online. What kind of picture is considered inappropriate varies from family to family and their own value systems. It is neither my place nor my intent to tell anybody outside of my own family what types of pictures cross that line. However there is one thing that I can tell you: Once the picture finds its way onto the Internet, it's there to stay. There is no putting the genie back in the bottle on that one. I also know that the vast majority of younger people live in the here and now, giving little thought to the future. That revealing picture of your daughter when she was 16 years old will still be haunting her when she's in her twenties and beyond. As an adult, she might find such pictures a source of embarrassment with her new husband, her children, or her boss at work. I can't help but wonder in 5–10 years how many women will be regretting the pictures they allowed to be taken of themselves by their friends, at a senior trip or a college spring break. There is life beyond the here and now.

SOCIAL NETWORKING SITES

Social networking sites are all over the Internet. These are sites where friends and, more often, total strangers can go to meet in the cyberworld. I'm not talking here about sites such as LinkedIn, where professionals go to build a network of colleagues. I'm talking about social networking sites of a more casual nature, such as Facebook, TeenSpot, and MySpace. These online social networking sites are popular amongst teenagers and the twentysomething crowd. Perhaps one of the most popular ones out there is YouTube. I can hear the protestors now. "Wait a moment—there's a bunch of really good information on these sites, particularly YouTube." In all frankness, the protestors are correct. YouTube does contain a lot of informational videos. My cautionary word is the same as for other such sites: There aren't strong restrictions governing the type of content that children can see or post on these sites. With these types of social networking sites, you can create your own profile, post pictures or videos, and have chats with others in your online social networking community. Again, once a picture or a video is posted online, there's no getting it back. Even if you're able to remove an item from the site itself, consider how many have viewed the pictures or video and have subsequently downloaded it onto their own home computers. As mentioned, there is no putting that genie back in the bottle. To make matters worse, it doesn't take any real in-depth computer knowledge to be able to post pictures on a social networking site such as YouTube. All you need is a digital camera with a USB cable, and access to a computer that is connected to the Internet. That's knowledge and access that most teenagers of today have.

MATCHMAKING SITES

There are other social networking sites geared more towards adults, people looking to meet that "special someone." Sites such as Match.com and eHarmony.com match adults looking for companionship, a relation-ship, and even marriage. As mature adults, we are better able to protect ourselves when we're interacting with total strangers. However, akin to blind dates of the past, people should still be cautious when getting together with somebody that they've met online. I would recommend the first date being in a public place, perhaps for lunch or even just a cup of coffee.

CHILDREN AND CHAT ROOMS

Perhaps even more dangerous than posting risqué pictures on social networking sites are the chat rooms. Such sites are frequented by adult sexual predators often posing as teenagers themselves. You hear the stories in the news all the time. A young teen goes to meet a person whom she met online and who told her he was her own age. They arrange to meet at a local mall for a "play date," and that youngster who's supposed to be her same age is in reality a predatory adult. This is not a risk limited to girls; young boys are in danger as well. For pedophiles, and those belonging to groups such as the Man-Boy Love Association, such social networking sites are fertile territory to try to lure youngsters for their own ends.

Sometimes I get odd looks when I advise parents to monitor their children's activities in chat rooms. Consider this: Would you allow your child to have a telephone conversation with a total stranger, or would you intervene? A chat room can be even more dangerous because on the phone, it's harder for a 45-year-old adult to pose as a 15-year-old child.

To help ensure a certain degree of safety into your child's chat room experience, you can insist that they chat only with people that they know— more specifically, other kids that they know in the "real world." You see, it's one thing to meet somebody that you know in the real world in the cyber-world. That has much less risk associated with it. However, it is extremely dangerous for a child to allow somebody they met in the cyberworld into their real world. Of course, a child predator that your child knows in the "real world" can also use a chat room as part of the grooming process on the road to abusing children. Spot check your children's chat room sessions. Tell them that they should be chatting only with their friends, kids their own age.

You should also have your kids tell their friends that you're monitoring what goes on in their chat rooms. This will discourage any tendencies towards inappropriate behavior. On a less threatening level, there are also issues of cheating on tests, swearing, and talking ill of teachers or classmates. While certainly not as serious a situation protecting our children from child predators, they are still situations that should be discouraged.

The threats of social networking sites are real, and can even be deadly. There are numerous sad cases of "cyberbullying" that end in suicide or attempted suicide. One victim, Megan, was befriended and then cyberbullied to the point where this young teen, with her whole life ahead of her, committed suicide. And guess what? The cyberbully, "16-year-old" Josh Evans, was, in fact, an adult.

It's up to us as parents to educate our children about such dangers. There are some things that we can do to help not only educate, but also protect our children.

1. Tell your children to never, ever provide personal information online.

That includes things such as their full names, what school they attend, what city they live in, the name of the high school basketball team they play on, and more. To illustrate their point, as part of a school-sponsored awareness campaign, police officers have started going into chat rooms and gaining seemingly vague information from children. Both the kids and parents are stunned when these cybercops show up at their school, knowing exactly who the youngsters are. Tell your children that if a stranger in a chat room asks them for personal information, *just say no*. Also, advise your kids that they should tell you right away if somebody says something in a chat room that makes them feel uncomfortable. It's important to bear in mind that in most cases, you're interacting with total strangers in chat rooms. It's also important to realize that in most cases, chat rooms are not monitored by the company that is providing the interactive forum.

2. Know what sites your children are going to on the Internet.

It's up to us as parents to be involved in our children's Web surfing. Don't give into the peer pressure when your kid tells you, "But mom, everybody else in school is on MySpace." It's not my intention to bash social networking sites. Rather, I am promoting strong parenting. In my house, my kids are not allowed on such sites, and I really don't care if other parents let their kids go there or not. In my house, my kids live by the rules set by my wife and me, and not by their friends. I will say that some of these sites do have their positive sides. YouTube does have some pretty clever and entertaining videos on its site. Just as if my son wanted to go a PG-13- or R-rated movie, either my wife or I, or an adult whom we knew and trusted, would have to see the video first to determine if it's appropriate for him to watch. Videos on sites such as YouTube are no different. If I seem to be holding a rather strict line, it might be that I'm just more aware of the dangers because of the profession that I'm in. In addition to my computer background, I am also a former police officer. I am painfully aware of the evil that certain people are capable of.

There are, in fact, a number of more kid-friendly sites available on the Internet. I feel safer letting my kids surf Web sites such as Disney.com and NickJr.com more so than a social networking site better suited for mature adults. Even with those types of Web sites, a certain degree of parental oversight would still be prudent. Many sites will ask visitors to set up a user account. If for no other reason than to not wanting to be barraged by e-mails touting the latest and greatest offers from the various sites, I recommend placing reasonable restrictions on your child's ability to establish online user accounts. So, another rule in the Alexander household is that if they need to set up a user account, they need to get permission first, and then they are to use their first names only.

3. Limit when your children can go online.

Does the concept of limiting your child's online computer usage sound far out? Consider that when we were growing up, many of our parents limited our TV-watching time. As adults, we now realize that limiting our time sitting in front of the "boob tube" was for our own good. So is placing reasonable limits on our kid's Internet usage. I'm not talking about doing conducting online research as part of a homework project, but rather playing online games, social networking, etc. What time limits are appropriate? That's a personal issue. Depending on your comfort level, you may consider limiting your child's Internet usage to when a parent is home. Just as there are programs on the television today that we don't want our kids to watch, there are sites on the Internet we don't want them to visit. To ensure a healthy balance, consider limiting the amount of time your kids can be online. While there was only so much danger in my playing too much Ms. Pacman or Donkey Kong, my parents wanted to see me outside playing with my friends as well. The same concept applies to kids spending too much time in front of the computer. Sitting in front of a computer surfing the Web does not constitute physical exercise. Exercise is, rather, running, jumping, and playing. Not only is exercise important, but it's a good way to fight the child obesity problem that we have in the United States.

4. Have frank discussions with your children.

Remember the old saying, "You can't trust anybody over 30"? Well, that hasn't changed too much. It's important to understand that many kids will place more stock in what their friends tell them than in what we as parents tell them. Even with that often-uneven playing field, if we don't have tough discussions with our children, their only source of information will be the playground.

So, it is important to have open and frank discussions with our children about the dangers of such sites. Now, discussions about pedophiles and sex crimes are not comfortable topics. The level of detail and the delivery method of such topics are very personal and must be couched in what you consider appropriate for your family. You also need to take into account the level of maturity that you believe your child has and what they can handle. It's the hard balance of not wanting to rob them of their childhood innocence, while informing them of the dangers that are out there in the world. When considering what type of conversation is appropriate, bear in mind that nothing will rob them of their innocence more quickly than being victimized by a child sexual predator.

5. Trust, but verify.

Right about now, you are sensing that I'm going to talk about spying on our kids. You are right. The truth of the matter is that many kids will be tempted to go to sites that we've declared off limits because they think we're not hip. Perhaps one of the oldest reasons in the world that most of us used when we were kids is, "But mom, everybody else is doing it." Just as the issue of having tough talks with our kids about the dangers of social networking sites is very personal, so is the issue of when spying on our children is the right thing to do. Consider this: When your child tells you that he is going out, do you ask where and with whom? Do you set a curfew? If they say that they're going to a movie, do you ask what they are going to see? In the age of cable television, do you put any restrictions on what they're allowed to watch?

I also suggest that parents consider reading their child's e-mails. Again, I realize this is a very sensitive area; but as a parent, it's our job to keep our children safe. I need to know if either of my kids are having e-mail conversations with strangers. For that matter, I also want to know if they're carrying on e-mail conservations with kids they know but that are of an inappropriate nature. My two sons know my feelings about swearing (using the "f" word, for example), talking disrespectfully about adults, or having conversations that are of a demeaning/sexual nature towards women. I don't approve of such conduct, in conversations or in e-mails.

Cyberbullying is also a real threat, so I want to protect my children from being victimized as well. I understand that this type of invasion of privacy is a very sensitive issue. Bear in mind that it is very common for businesses to have a policy that allows management to read the e-mails that employees send and receive from their work e-mail accounts. Companies need to protect their employees and themselves from issues such as sexual harassment, inappropriate humor, and threatening e-mails.

What precisely is the appropriate balance between respecting your child's right to privacy and snooping enough for their own good is a tough question. Again, I believe that the decision is best left up to the parents. We know our kids best. I would caution about choosing either extreme. Too much "spying," and you risk alienating your child and having them rebel against you. Take too much of what can be called a "hands-off" approach, and you might not know they're in trouble online until it's too late. Again, sexual predators are out there. It's important to keep in mind that in most cases, they are not the evil-looking man with a handlebar mustache wearing dark clothing like you might see in an old Western on television. The hard truth is that in most cases, they are people whom we know in the community, in our schools, and in our places of worship. Sexual predators place themselves in a position of trust that also involves access to children. Now, not all adults who work around children are sexual predators. As parents, we need to educate our children about what behavior is appropriate, and to be involved in their lives so that we can stop a bad situation from ever starting.

There are companies that provide services to help parents in their quest to keep their kids safe online. They allow parents to both control and monitor their children's online activities. I've placed a list of a number of such companies, along with their Web sites, in Appendix B. I want to stress that these sites would serve as an augmentation to responsible parental oversight, and not as a substitution for it.

Another thing you can do to help deter your children from engaging in inappropriate activities online is to place the computer in an open place within your home. While mom and dad might have a television in their bedroom, it is not uncommon for many families to have their "main" television in a shared family room within their home. Many families will also not let their younger children have a television in their own bedroom for a number of reasons. Some of the reasons include not wanting it to interfere with homework, or to keep children from spending too much time in front of the television. Another reason is to be able to better monitor what our children are watching. With the advent of cable television and premium channels such as HBO and Showtime, there are a whole range of offerings available on the small screen today, some of which we might not want our children exposed to. While many televisions have the technology to enact parental controls to block certain programs, perhaps the best form of control is effective parental supervision. I also realize that many popular electronic games today such as the Wii and GameCube require a television. What I've done is place a television in my older son's room so that he can play his games. The television is not connected to our cable service, so it is strictly a gaming monitor; he can't watch television programs on it. Again, it's not that I don't trust my kids; I do. It's a parenting style that my wife and I practice. You can also opt to purchase a computer monitor instead of a television for your kids to play their electronic games on. As long as they have the appropriate input, and most do, they'll work just fine.

LOOK FOR THE SIGNS

One of the cornerstones of effective parental supervision is to be on the lookout for signs that your child might be engaged in inappropriate behavior online. Similar to taking drugs or other activities that your kids know deep down are wrong, there will be signs—some subtle, some not—that they're trying to hide things from you. Here are some things to look for.

- You find pornography on the family home computer.
- You notice an unexplained loss of available hard drive space.
- You see unfamiliar icons on your desktop.
- You start getting e-mail solicitations to join sex sites.
- You start getting e-mail solicitations to join social networking sites.
- You start receiving telephone calls from strangers asking to speak to your child.
- Your child is making phone calls to total strangers.
- Your child is spending an inordinate amount of time online in front of the computer (especially if this overshadows other previously popular activities such as sports or playing with his or her friends).
- You find e-mails from total strangers who know a lot of personal (intimate) information about your child as well as other members of your family.
- Your child abruptly turns off the computer monitor when you approach.
- Your child abruptly closes an e-mail when you approach.
- Your child abruptly closes the Internet browser window when you approach.
- Your child starts using a friend's e-mail account.
- You find that your child has created an e-mail account for themselves without your knowledge.

In addition to these telltale signs, there are things that you can do to check for signs that your child may be engaging in inappropriate activity online. Internet Web browsers, such as Microsoft's Internet Explorer (IE), keep a record of the sites that have been visited. The window at the top of IE which displays what site we are on, keeps that history. It has a drop-down arrow that is located on the lower right corner of the window. Simply click on the arrow to see what sites have been visited. This way you can know if any sites that you have deemed inappropriate have been visited. Explorer also has an "auto-complete" feature on sites stored in its history. So, if you're going to Hotmail and, upon typing "hot," "hot girls" comes up, that means that a site has been visited that might not meet with your approval.

IE can be configured to retain browsing history for up to 99 days in IE version 6, and up to 999 days in version 7. For both versions, go to Tools and then Internet Options to access the browser history settings. Now, while

999 days of browsing history does seem a little excessive, consider a number around 30 days as a more reasonable initial setting. Both versions of Internet Explorer also allow for the deletion of the browser history, overriding the predefined retention period. So, if you have configured Internet Explorer to keep a history for 30 days, and when you check, you find it's blank, you'll know that somebody has purposely deleted the file. That would also be a possible indication that your child is trying to erase the evidence of where they've been online.

Another way to see what sites your children have visited is by looking in the Temporary Internet Files folder. That is the default location where cookies are stored. Many Web sites will install a small file known as a tracking cookie on your computer as a way for them to remember that you've visited their particular site. As with the browsing history, if upon checking your computer's Temporary Internet Files folder, you see that it is empty that's yet another possible indication of somebody trying to conceal where they've been on the Internet.

Content Advisor, which is a part of part of Internet Explorer, can be configured to block sites based on a number of categories, including language, nudity, sex, and violence. In IE version 6, each category has settings ranging from level 0 up to level 4. Table 11.1 lists the different levels available in Content Advisor, and their respective descriptions for IE version 6, while Table 11.2 is for IE version 7.

Table 11.1
Internet Explorer 6—Content Advisor Settings

Level	0	1	2	3	4
Language	Inoffensive language	Mild expletives	Moderate gestures	Obscene gestures	Explicit or crude language
Nudity	None	Revealing attire	Partial nudity	Frontal nudity	Provocative frontal nudity
Sex	None	Passionate kissing	Clothed sexual touching	Non-explicit sexual touching	Explicit sexual activity
Violence	No violence	Fighting	Killing	Killing with blood and gore	Wanton and gratuitous violence

Table 11.2
Internet Explorer 7—Content Advisor Settings

Level	0	1	2	3
Content that creates fear, intimidation, etc.	No content that creates feelings of fear, intimidation, etc., in any context.	Content that creates feelings of fear, intimidation, etc., only in artistic, medical, educational, sports, or news context.	Content that creates feelings of fear, intimidation, etc., in any context.	
Content that sets a bad example for young people	No content that sets a bad example for young children, teaching or encouraging children to perform harmful acts or imitate dangerous behaviors in any context.	Content that sets a bad example for young children, teaching or encouraging children to perform harmful acts or imitate dangerous behaviors, in artistic, medical, educational, sports, or news context only.	Content that sets a bad example for young children, teaching or encouraging children to perform harmful acts or imitate dangerous behaviors, in any context.	
Depiction of alcohol	No depiction of alcohol use in any context.	Depiction of alcohol use only in artistic, medical, educational, sports, or news context.	Depiction of alcohol use in any context.	
Depiction of drug use	No depiction of drug use in any context.	Depiction of drug use only in artistic,	Depiction of drug use in any context.	

Table 11.2 (continued)

Level	0	1	2	3
		medical, educational, sports, or news context.		
Depiction of gambling	No depiction of gambling in any context.	Depiction of gambling only in artistic, medical, educational, or news context.	Depiction of gambling in any context.	
Depiction of tobacco use	No depiction of tobacco use in any context.	Depiction of tobacco use only in artistic, medical, educational, sports, or news context.	Depiction of tobacco use in any context.	
Depiction of weapon use	No depiction of weapon use in any context.	Depiction of weapon use only in artistic, medical, educational, sports, or news context.	Depiction of weapon use in any context.	
Incitement/ depiction of discrimination or harm	No incitement/ depiction of discrimination or harm in any context.	Incitement/ depiction of discrimination or harm in artistic, medical, educational, sports, or news context only.	Incitement/ depiction of discrimination or harm in any context.	
Language	No abusive or vulgar terms, no profanity or swearing, no mild	No abusive or vulgar terms in any context. Profanity, swearing, or	Abusive or vulgar terms only in artistic, medical,	Abusive or vulgar terms, profanity, swearing, or mild expletives

Level	0	1	2	3
	expletives in any context.	mild expletives only in artistic, medical, educational, sports, or news context.	educational, sports, or news context. Crude words, profanity, or mild expletives in any context.	in any context, although this does not include sexual language, which is described separately.
Nudity	No bare buttocks, breasts, or genitals in any context.	Bare buttocks and/or bare breasts in artistic, medical, educational, sports, or news context. No genitals in any context.	Bare buttocks and/or bare breasts in artistic, medical, educational, sports, or news context. No genitals in any context.	Nudity of any kind in any context, although this does not imply sexual content, which is described separately.
Sexual material	No passionate kissing, obscured or implied sexual acts, visible sexual touching, explicit sexual language, erections, explicit sexual acts, or erotica in any context.	Obscured or implied sexual acts and visible sexual touching in an artistic, medical, educational, sports, or news context. Passionate kissing in any context. No explicit sexual content in any context.	Obscured or implied sexual acts, visible sexual touching, and passionate kissing in any context. Explicit sexual context or erotica in artistic, medical, educational, sports or news context only.	Sexual material of any kind, in any context, although this does not include sexual violence, which is described separately.

Table 11.2 (continued)

Level	0	1	2	3
User-generated content	No user-generated content, such as chat rooms and message boards, in any context.	Moderated user-generated content, such as chat rooms and message boards, in any context.	Moderated user-generated content in any context. Unmoderated user-generated content only in artistic, medical, educational, sports, or news context.	Unmoderated user-generated content, such as chat rooms and message boards, in any context.
Violence	No assault/rape; no injury, torture, killing, or blood and dismemberment of humans, animals, or fantasy characters (including animation) in any context.	Injury, torture, killing, or blood and dismemberment of fantasy characters only in artistic, medical, educational, sports, or news context. None of the aforementioned of humans or animals in any context. No assault/rape.	Injury, torture, killing, or blood and dismemberment of fantasy characters in any context. That of humans or animals in artistic, medical, educational, sports, or news context only. No assault/rape.	Violence of any kind in any context, including assault/rape.

As you can see, Microsoft greatly expanded the Content Advisor in version 7 of Internet Explorer. You'll also note that some of the categories have three levels, while others have a fourth. In both versions 6 and 7, moving up the levels from the various categories, you get more graphic, or some would say more adult, content. You can set the Content Advisor at whatever levels you are comfortable with and what you feel is appropriate for your children. Since the main way that online predators attempt to gain access to minors is through chat rooms, Microsoft's "User-generated content" settings in version 7 is a good one to utilize to block your kids from using them.

There are a few unfortunate limitations to the Content Advisor filtering capability. First of all, it is up to the individual Web site owners to honestly and accurately rank their own sites, or even to rate them at all. So, the very people showing what many would deem offensive content are being asked to honestly rate their own sites to help us keep our children from going there. Content Advisor does, however, have a check box asking if you want to be able to see sites that aren't rated. The problem with this is that so many sites don't rate themselves. The first time I tested that functionality for myself, I was blocked from accessing my home page, which for me is "My Yahoo." Trust me, there's no sex, nudity, or any other kind of adult content there. So if you don't allow the visiting of unrated Web sites, you will so severely limit the ability to use the Internet as to make it almost unusable.

Secondly, while both Windows XP and Windows Vista allow for multiple user profiles, the settings in Content Advisor for one user will be applied to all. In effect, you'll be placing the same limits on your own Web browsing that you place on your children. Content Advisor does allow for an override password in order to visit blocked sites. It would be important, then, not to share the password with your kids, as that would negate the limitations you're trying to set by using Content Advisor in the first place. You can also use the Content Advisor password to disable it while you're using it. It would then require that you re-enable it again prior to your children accessing the computer.

Even placing all the settings to zero, which is the most restrictive, I was still able to visit questionable sites. For example, even with the "Depiction of Drug Use" rating on its most limited setting, I was able to visit sites on how to make drugs such as methamphetamines. The sites didn't depict people using meth, but did describe how to manufacture the drug. So, with these limitations, my advice here then is to realize that Content Advisor is just one tool that we as parents can use to help keep our children safe online. It is not a substitute for appropriate parental supervision.

If you run a small business, this type of content filtering may also be appropriate. In this day and age, we must be sensitive to the fact that what somebody might find funny may very well be offensive to somebody else. Enabling Content Advisor on your employees' workstations and laptops will limit what sites they can visit as well. Even with its technical limitations, enabling such filtering will show that your company doesn't condone accessing such sites. Of course, having a written policy about appropriate Internet usage on company computers is also a very good idea. After all, you don't want to pay your employees for playing poker online or spending hours in chat rooms.

BLOCK OUTGOING DATA

Many software firewall programs on the market today have data-blocking features. They can be configured to not allow certain pieces of data from being sent from your computer. Consider blocking personally identifiable information such as Social Security numbers, your credit card account numbers, your family surname, and the name of the school your child attends. Obviously, the list of data elements can get rather long, depending on your personal preferences. Consider an added level of security by truncating the data you place on your "to be blocked" list. For instance, instead of placing your entire Social Security number on your computers' data block list, only place the last four digits. This will still block your Social Security number from being sent from your computer, without requiring that you actually enter the entire number. That way, if your computer does get hacked, the bad guy won't have your entire Social Security number and be able to steal your identity. The same technique would work for entering in partial credit card account numbers, checking account numbers, and so forth. Many such programs require that a password be entered in order to allow a piece of information to be sent that is on the blocked list. Thus, as the parent, you could enter your credit card account number for making online purchases while still blocking your kids from releasing sensitive data such as the name of the school they attend.

THE NUMBERS ARE STAGGERING

There's one point I want to make very clear: The risks that online predators pose to our kids is very real. Ignorance is not bliss, nor is the mind-set that leads people to believe that this is only a problem that affects other people. If you feel that such problems affect only kids from other families and that your son or daughter certainly wouldn't engage in risky online behavior, then I ask you to look at the following sobering statistics. The National Center for Missing and Exploited Children, along with Cox Communication and national child advocate John Walsh have sponsored annual surveys of children's behavior online. The surveys themselves were conducted by Teenage Research Unlimited. The following numbers,[1] which are from their most recent survey, serve to remind all of us of the gravity of this problem. One could even say that the numbers are staggering.

Teens are increasingly active online and at potential risk of falling prey to online predators.

- A large majority of teens (71 percent) have established online profiles (including those on social networking sites such as MySpace, Friendster, and Xanga), up from 61 percent in 2006.
- Sixty-nine percent of teens regularly receive personal messages online from people they don't know, and most of them don't tell a trusted adult about it.
- Teens readily post personal info online; 64 percent post photos or videos of themselves, while more than half (58 percent) post info about where they live. Female teens are far more likely than male teens to post personal photos or videos of themselves (70 percent vs. 58 percent).
- Nearly one in 10 teens (8 percent) has posted his or her cell phone number online.
- Overall, 19 percent of teens report they have been harassed or bullied online, and the incidence of online harassment is higher (23 percent) among 16- and 17-year-olds. Girls are more likely to be harassed or bullied than boys (21 percent vs. 17 percent).

Parents and guardians are becoming more involved in monitoring their teens' Internet use and talking to them about online safety.

- Parental awareness of their teens' online activities has risen significantly. In 2007, 25 percent of teens say their parents know "little" or "nothing" about what they do online, down from 33 percent the previous year.
- Forty-one percent of teens report their parents talk to them "a lot" about Internet safety (up five points over 2006), and three out of four say their parents have talked to them in the past year about the potential dangers of posting personal info. The level of parental involvement is higher for younger teens and girls, although it has increased across all age groups and both genders.
- Teens whose parents have talked to them "a lot" about Internet safety are more concerned about the risks of sharing personal info online than teens whose parents are less involved. For instance, 65 percent of those whose parents have not talked to them about online safety post info about where they live compared to 48 percent of teens with more involved parents.

- Teens whose parents have talked to them "a lot" about online safety are less likely to consider meeting face to face with someone they met on the Internet (12 percent vs. 20 percent).

Many teens are unconcerned about the dangers of sharing personal info online.

- A majority of teens (58 percent) don't think posting photos or other personal info on social networking sites is unsafe.
- Nearly half of teens (47 percent) aren't worried about others using their personal info in ways they don't want (although that represents a 10-percentage-point improvement over 2006).
- About half (49 percent) are unconcerned that posting personal info online might negatively affect their future.

Teens are showing some signs of making safer, smarter choices online.

- While 16 percent of teens say they've considered meeting face to face with someone they've talked to only online, that marks a significant drop compared to the 30 percent of teens who were considering such a meeting in 2006. In 2007, 8 percent of teens say they actually have met in person with someone from the Internet, down from 14 percent in 2006.
- When they receive online messages from someone they don't know, 60 percent of teens say they usually respond only to ask who the person is. Compared to the 2006 survey, there was a 10-percentage-point increase in teens ignoring such messages (57 percent vs. 47 percent). Still, nearly a third of teens (31 percent) say they usually reply and chat with people they don't know, and only 21 percent tell a trusted adult when they receive such messages

KNOWLEDGE IS POWER

I know firsthand that kids, particularly teenagers, will insist that many Web sites are fine. My recommendation to you is that when in doubt, check it out. It is not uncommon for parents to preview a movie when they are not certain whether or not it is appropriate for their kids before letting them see it. The obvious reason is that there is a large variance among PG-13- and R-rated movies and the kind of "adult" content and concepts that they can contain. Web sites are no different; in essence, they can even be worse. At least with movies, there is the Motion Picture Association of America to rate them. We can go to G- and PG-rated movies with a degree of certainty there won't be any offensive content. Likewise, movies rated R and higher will undoubtedly contain adult content of one kind or another. Keep in mind that, aside from the obvious "adult" sites with sexually explicit names, many seemingly innocent sites may actually contain what for you may be considered objectionable behavior. For example, TeenWire.com, by its name could indicate a Web site that talks about topics specific to teenagers, such as the latest fashions, the latest rock-and-roll band, who's winning on *American Idol,* and more. In reality, TeenWire.com is a site that discusses adult issues, including sexual techniques, oral sex, gay sex, transgender issues, schoolage kids having sex, and more. Do you really want your 13-year-old son or daughter reading about sexual techniques online?

As a teenager back in the late 1970s, the most provocative material I ever hoped to get my hands on was a *Playboy* magazine. *Playboy* is tame by today's standards, especially when you consider what kids can be exposed to online. What's more, you'd have to build up the nerve to buy a *Playboy* magazine from a convenience store clerk, whom you were afraid would tell your parents. Now, there are few barriers to such material.

I do not want to close this chapter leaving you thinking that there aren't any good Web sites out there. There are Web sites on the Internet that are geared towards children and that don't contain any adult content. Sites from well-known companies such as Disney, Nickelodeon, and others provide Internet experiences that are safe, fun, and, in many instances, even educational. There are also sites that are very educational, such as, literacy.org for reading, kidsnumbers.com for mathematics, and more. The good stuff is out there; sometimes, it just takes a bit of effort on our part to guide our children to them.

SUMMARY

We have come to the end of what I sincerely hope has been an informative book for you. The incredible advances in technology have given all of us unprecedented access to information. Unfortunately, it has also introduced hazards that didn't exist in the pre-Internet era. If you come away with information that can help you safeguard yourself, your children, or your business in this electronic age that we live in, then I have met my goal. I also want to extend a personal thank you for taking the time to read my book. Everybody's time is valuable, and I hope you consider the time spent reading my book as time well spent.

NOTE

1. *Source:* TRU, the leading youth-focused market-research firm. http://www.tru-insight.com/. Used with permission.

Appendix A

Online Backup Services

For many small and home-based businesses, as well as home computer networks, utilizing an online backup server is the preferred method. The security is "good enough," and it removes the burden of developing and administering your own backup regimen. The following list, while certainly not all-inclusive, does provide the names of a wide range of companies that provide online backup services. I've listed these companies strictly as a resource to assist you. I still advise that you do your homework before choosing any of these, or a company that is not listed, prior to signing up to use the service. They all vary with regard to price, the amount of data that they'll allow you to back up, and, of course, the level of customer service.

Backup.com
http://www.backup.com/

BackupNation.com
http://www.backupnation.com/

Backup Right
http://www.backupright.com

Backup Solutions
http://www.backuphelp.com/

Carbonite
http://www.carbonite.com/

Data Deposit Box
http://www.datadepositbox.com

Data Protection Services
http://www.dataprotection.com/

Dr. Backup
http://www.drbackup.net

Homeland Data Security, LLC
http://www.hdsbackup.com/home.asp

IBackup
http://www.ibackup.com/ibackup-for-windows/

IDrive
http://www.idrive.com

Intronis Technologies
http://www.intronis.com

Mozy
http://www.mozy.com

NovaStor
http://us.novastor.com

Professional Offsite Data Backup Inc.
http://www.backmeupoffsite.net

Rhinoback
http://www.rhinoback.com/

Storage Guardian
http://www.storageguardian.com

SyncWeb Data Backup
http://www.syncweb.net/

Vembu
http://www.vembu.com/

SERVICES TO HELP KEEP CHILDREN SAFER ONLINE

The following is a list of Web sites that contain a wealth of useful information on how to keep our children safe while they are online. Many also offer products that are designed to help parents keep their children safe while they are surfing the World Wide Web. Some sites also have software that will allow parents the ability to see what sites their children are visiting. I realize that this is a sensitive area. It is up to each and every one of us to determine precisely what level of oversight is appropriate. That said, I believe that knowledge is power. It's with that in mind, and with a sincere desire to make sure that our kids have a safe Internet experience, that I've listed the following Web sites.

4Safe
http://4safe.com/yahoo/?kword=parentalcontrol

bSafeOnline
  http://bsafehome.com/

Christian Broadband.com
http://www.christianbroadband.com/

Content Purity
http://www.contentpurity.com/

Cyber Patrol
  http://www.cyberpatrol.com/

Cyber Sitter
http://www.cybersitter.com/

Federal Bureau of Investigation
  http://www.fbi.gov/publications/pguide/pguidee.htm

iSafe
http://www.isafe.org/

Kids Watch Parental Computer Control
http://www.kidswatch.com/

National Crime Prevention Council—Cyberbullying
http://www.ncpc.org/cyberbullying

NetLingo
http://www.netlingo.com/

NetSmartz
http://www.netsmartz.org/

Parental Control Toolbar
http://www.parentalcontrolbar.org/

PC Tattletale
http://www.pctattletale.com/

Phantom Technologies
http://residential.iphantom.com/

Sentry Parental Controls
http://www.sentryparentalcontrols.com/

SnoopStick
http://www.snoopstick.com/

SpectorSoft
http://www.spectorsoft.com/

Web Watcher
http://www.awarenesstech.com/Parental/

WiredKids
http://www.wiredkids.org/

TIPS AND TRICKS

've put together a list of quick "tips and tricks." Keeping with the theme of my book, there are things you can do to protect your computer, your identity, and most importantly, your kids.

1. Phishing and spyware
   a. Only click "yes" to things when you know what the outcome will be.
   b. Don't click links that ask you to provide personal information.
   c. Don't download programs from companies you're not familiar with.
2. Identity theft
   a. Be careful disclosing sensitive personal information online, such as last name, Social Security number, home address, phone number, and checking/savings account numbers.
   b. Closely monitor your finances and watch your credit report. You can order a free credit report once every 12 months. (See http://www.annualcreditreport.com.)
3. Responsibility
   a. Don't write down your user/ID and password.
   b. Password-protect your desktop/laptop while unattended.
4. Passwords
   a. Don't use blank passwords.
   b. Choose a password that's both easy to remember and hard to guess. Consider using a pass phrase, such as; **I** Love **My** **W**ife **C**ency **V**ery **M**uch. The password would be ILMWCVM.
   c. Don't write passwords down (taped to the bottom of a laptop).
   d. Don't share passwords.
5. Malware
   a. Be aware of the threat.
   b. Update your antivirus and antispyware regularly (use an auto-update feature if your program has one).

    c. Never open e-mail attachments from unknown senders, and always scan before downloading even if it's from a known sender.

6. Telecommuting/home working and remote access
    a. Use a personal firewall (hardware or software).
    b. Use encryption when transmitting data over the Internet. (All VPN software includes encryption. If you're using an Internet-based user access service, make certain it encrypts data while it's in transit.)
7. Email hoaxes
    a. Add the sender's address to your e-mail program's blocked senders list.
    b. Delete them.
    c. Don't forward them.
8. Instant messaging
    a. Don't discuss secrets or illicit material over Internet-based IM.
    b. Don't send personal information over an Internet-based IM session.
    c. Update your IM software regularly.
9. Firewalls and patches
    a. Use a personal firewall.
    b. Patch the system at regular intervals.
    c. Update your antivirus regularly.
10. PDAs
    a. Physically secure them.
    b. Use passwords and encryption.
    c. Disable wireless auto connection.
11. Internet use—(work)
    a. Minimize personal use.
    b. Avoid use of Internet-based IM.
    c. Have a policy forbidding employees from visiting inappropriate sites (pornography, gambling, etc.).
    d. Don't download unapproved software onto your work workstation/laptop.
12. Protecting your Children Online
    a. Have frank discussions with your kids about Internet safety.
    b. Monitor your kids' Internet usage, e-mail, and instant messaging.
    c. Tell your children that you will be monitoring their computer activity.
    d. Check the browsing history on your computer to see where your children are going online.

e. Have age appropriate discussions with your kids about "stranger danger," being cautious with people they "meet" online, and cyber-bullying.

f. Let your kids know that they are to come to you if ever they're made to feel uncomfortable online (in a chat room/IM) or if they're asked to provide personal information about themselves.

g. Tell your kids to not allow a stranger that they met in the cyber-world into their real world (no play dates with people they've met online).

GLOSSARY

Administrator Account: A type of user account on a computer generally reserved to support personnel charted with maintaining the system. On Windows-based servers, an administrator account is capable of performing any task.

Adware: Software that has an advertising function integrated into it. Usually associated with software that is given aware for free, but that seeks voluntary donations from users. Generally used by programmers as a way to recover some of the costs of developing the program in the first place.

AES: Short for Advanced Encryption Standard, which was developed by a mathematician named Rijndael, and is the current encryption standard used by many private companies as well as governmental agencies to protect the confidentiality of sensitive data.

Analog or analogue: Any variable signal continuous in both time and amplitude. This differs from digital signals, which are either on or off. In the context of network data transmissions, analog is generally associated with using modems. Analog is also susceptible to interference from outside noise. Similar to having a "bad" connection with telephone conservations, analog network data transmissions can suffer from background noise as well.

Biometrics: A type of authentication based on what you are. Biometrics is considered more difficult to hack than a password, since biometric indicators are specific to each person. Also, it's much easier to guess somebody's password than it is to copy their fingerprints. Aside from fingerprints, other commonly used forms of biometrics include voice prints, palm prints, and retina scans.

Bits: A binary value that must be mutually exclusive, such as true/false, yes/no, or, in computer terms, expressed as either a 0 or a 1. As a base level, computers read information in binary, consisting of millions of 0s and 1s.

Bluejacking: The act of sending unwanted messages to a Bluetooth device, such as a cell phone or a PDA. It can also include unsolicited messages akin to junk mail.

Bluesnarfing: The act of obtaining unauthorized access to information being transmitted between two Bluetooth-enabled devices, such as cell phones or PDAs.

The data can include contact lists, calendars, and even e-mails and text messages. A defense against Bluesnarfing is to set your device to "hidden" rather than "discoverable."

Bluetooth: An industry standard for short-range wireless networks, also known as personal area networks. Bluetooth technology is commonly used with mobile phones, laptops, printers, digital cameras, and more.

Bytes: Are the equivalent of eight bits of data. "01101001" is an example of a byte.

Caesar Cipher: Named after both Julius and Augustus Caesar, the Caesar Cipher is a substitution cipher. While the actual implementation of the Caesar Cipher did vary somewhat from Julius to Augustus, they both worked off of the same principle of substituting letters and numbers for the actual values in order to safely send information to their soldiers in the field. Their soldiers would then decipher the code in order to reveal the actual message.

Chat Room: A term used to describe many forms of online conferencing. They can be either public or private and are most commonly used on social networking sites.

Cookies: Also known as tracking cookies, these are small pieces of data sent to your computer generally from an Internet site to help the site track that you've been there.

Cyberbullying: Unlike the playground bullying that has gone on in schools for decades, cyberbullying takes place strictly online. The bullying can take place via e-mail, through instant messages, or in chat rooms. Cyberbullying can be harder to spot than actual physical bullying, which is one of the factors that makes it so dangerous.

Demilitarized Zone (DMZ): In the context of computer networking, a DMZ denotes a segment of a network that is at a higher risk of attack. Generally placed near the outside perimeter of a company's computer network. Since computers within a DMZ are more susceptible to attack, they need to be configured to stricter security guidelines. It is also very common to have a firewall protecting the interior zone of a company's network from the DMZ.

Digital: Data transmissions that are either "on" or "off." Analog transmissions, on the other hand, are continuous at various frequencies. Most current-day data transmission lines in the United States use digital rather than analog.

Encryption: The mathematical process of alternating data and changing it into a form that is not understandable by the naked eye. The actual industry term is what is known as cipher text. Decryption is the reverse process. Encryption has been used for thousands of years to exchange data while protecting its confidentiality. The use of encryption goes all the way back to Julius Caesar, in what was called the Caesar Cipher. History tells up that Caesar employed a method of shifting letters three places to the left. For example, a "D" would be written as an "A." While considered easily broken by today's standards, it was likely very effective in Caesar's time. Consider that most of his enemies were not fluent in Latin, and even fewer had enough schooling to be able to read the written word.

Exploits: Weaknesses discovered in software such as operating systems and applications that a hacker can leverage to gain unauthorized access, steal data, or cause system interruptions. Software manufacturers will often issue fixes known as patches to fix exploits in their applications.

Firecall ID: Sometimes also referred to as a one-time-use password, these are passwords designed to be used only once and then discarded. They are thought to be nearly impossible to hack because of the one-time-use feature. The practice of utilizing one-time-use passwords have been used by armies in time of war as a way to protect access to sensitive information. In the private sector, firecall IDs are often used to provide emergency access to restricted systems. Reusing a firecall ID goes against the one-time-use model and lessens its effectiveness. In World War II, Germans began reusing their one-time-use IDs which made it possible for the Allies to compromise their systems.

Firewall: The term originally comes from the automobile industry, as there is a firewall in each car between the driver and the engine. The same concept is used in protecting your computer from the fires and explosions of the Internet. A firewall can be a piece of software that runs on your computer, or it can be a dedicated hardware device. In computer terms, then, a firewall sits between your computer, or your network, and the Internet.

Flux Capacitor: A fictional device that was made popular by the 1985 movie *Back to the Future*, released by Universal Pictures. Created by the movie's inventor character, Doctor Emmitt Brown, the flux capacitor made time travel possible.

Freeware: As the name entails, freeware is software that is available free of charge. Providers do sometimes solicit for optional donations. Keeping in line with the old adage "you get what you pay for," a certain amount of caution is called for with freeware. While some programs are quite good, others can harm your computer. Part of performing due diligence could well include performing online searches for reviews of the particular freeware before you decide to install it on your computer.

Gigabyte: A unit of information or computer storage equal to one billion bytes. It is commonly abbreviated "GB" and is the equivalent of 1,000 megabytes.

Graphical User Interface (GUI): A pictorial interface generally in the form of an icon, making many operations as easy as point and click. For example, printing a document is as easy as clicking on a icon that looks like a printer.

Hacker: A person engaged in malicious or even illegal activities, such as writing computer viruses attempting to break into computer systems to steal data, or to otherwise disrupt computer systems.

Hacking: The act of attempting to perform illegal, unauthorized, or unsolicited actions to computer systems. These acts can include the theft of data, defacing a Web site, or interrupting with the normal operations of a computer.

Hacktivism: A term given to a person who carries out hacking attacks against either a private-sector company or a government agency as part a particular social or political agenda.

Heisenberg Compensator: Made popular by the 1960s science fiction television series *Star Trek*, it is actually based on the real-life theorem called the Heisenberg Uncertainty Principle. This theorem states that it is not possible to determine both an atom's definite position as well as what it is doing at the same time. In *Star Trek*, the Heisenberg Compensator is supposed to have solved the problem of the Heisenberg Uncertainty Principle by compensating for any deviation in determining both an atom's precise location as well as what it is doing. This allows matter to be converted to energy and then back into matter again—and thus was born the transporter on the USS *Enterprise*.

Hub: Also referred to as a concentrator or a network hub, a device that is used for connecting multiple devices together on a computer network. A hub can accommodate different types of cabling, such as straight copper, twisted copper, and fiber optic. A hub can be used to connect computers as well as peripheral devices such as printers and fax machines.

Identity Theft: Occurs when somebody illegally acquires a person's personal data and then uses that information to commit a crime, such as fraud or theft. Identity theft can have disastrous results for the victim. The victim can find their credit ruined, or other crimes being perpetrated in their name.

ID/Fob: Generally a physical device, also known as a "token," that generates a number every 60 seconds and is used to provide PINs for authentication. Software ID/fobs are becoming more popular in recent years for use in cell phones and PDAs and are also less expensive then physical tokens.

Internet Service Provider (ISP): A company that provides access to the Internet. Today's ISPs may provide other related services as well, including antivirus, e-mail spam filters, and Web hosting. In the past, most ISPs were run by the phone companies, when people accessed the Internet via a dialup modem. Today, ISPs offer connectivity via cable modems or Digital Subscriber Lines (DSL).

Listening Ports: Also known as simply ports, these are openings for data connections on a computer that "listen" for data in order to accept it. Many well-known communications protocols used pre-identified listening ports. For example, Internet traffic generally uses either port 80 or 443. A common security hole in many computers occurs when unused listening ports are left open. Unused ports should be closed.

MAC Address: An alphanumeric value that is burned into a computer's network address card.

Malware: A generic term given to software that is specially designed to perform either harmful or unauthorized acts to computer systems. Specific types of malware include viruses, Trojans horses, spyware, and worms.

Megabit: A unit of measure that is most commonly used when referring to data transmission rates. Ethernet speeds, for example, can be set at 10, 100, or 1000 Mb/second.

Megabyte: Commonly abbreviated as "MB," a unit of information or computer storage equal to $1,024^2$ bytes.

Modem: A word derived from the terms (modulator-demodulator). A modem takes the digital signal from your computer and translates it to analog form to be sent over the phone line to the remote system. From there, the process is reversed, as the modem takes the incoming data in analog form and translates it back to digital so it can be understood by the computer.

Cable Modem: A type of modem that accesses the Internet by going over the cable television infrastructure. Cable modems are primarily used to deliver broadband Internet access in the form of cable Internet, taking advantage of unused bandwidth on a cable television network.

DSL Modem: DSL, which stands for Digital Subscriber Line, is medium for transferring data over regular phone lines. However, like a cable modem, a DSL circuit is much faster than a regular phone connection, even though the wires it uses are copper, like a typical phone line.

ISDN Modem: While not as fast as either a cable modem or a DSL modem, an ISDN modem is more than twice as fast as the "old-style" modems. If neither of the faster technologies, commonly referred to as broadband, are available in your area, ISDN may be your best bet.

Nigerian Scam: Also known as the "4-1-9" scam and the "Advance Fee Fraud Scheme," the Nigerian scam is a type of scam consisting of an e-mail promising huge payments for little to no work. The goal of the scammer is often to defraud people of a required transaction fee, or to steal their identity to commit financial fraud. The Nigerian scam got its name because many of the e-mails originate from Nigeria. However, today, they originate from just about anywhere.

Out-of-Wallet Questions: These are questions designed to be personal and hence easy to remember, but difficult for a hacker to guess. Common examples include your grandmother's maiden name, the town you were born in, and the color of your first car. Called out-of-wallet because this is information not generally written down and carried in either a purse or a wallet. Out-of-wallet questions are commonly used to help identify customers either online or over the phone when trying to access sensitive information such as credit card or banking account data.

Pager: Also known as a "beeper," the pager was invented by Multitone Electronics back in 1956 at St. Thomas' Hospital in London. While initially mainly used by doctors so they could be reached in the event of a medical emergency, they quickly become very popular and even trendy. The pager began to lose popularity with the invention of the cell phone.

Pass Phrase: Longer than a password, it generally consists of words found in normal speech. They are most effective when they are easy for the user to remember but still hard to guess. An example is a line from a favorite movie. For example "The flux capacitor is fluxing." It would become even harder to hack if altered slightly: "The flux capacitor I$ fluxing."

Password: A form of authentication, generally used in combination with a user ID to control access to an account. Passwords generally consist of a combination of numbers, lower case letters, upper case letters, and, for added security, a special character such as &, #, $, %, !, etc.

Patch: Software designed to fix problems with an application. A patch is often used to fix a security hole, but it can also improve usability in one way or another.

Personal Digital Assistant (PDA): A small electronic device that includes a number of the functions of a personal computer, including sending/receiving e-mail, texting, cell phone, music player, and digital camera.

Personal Identification Number (PIN): A series of numbers used to help identify a user for access. A PIN can either be static, only changing when done so by the user. An example of static PINs are ones used in order to gain access to your account at a bank's ATM. PINs can also be dynamic, changing every 60 seconds, as with ID/fobs. These are more commonly used as authentication for a Virtual Private Network.

Phishing: An attempt to fraudulently acquire sensitive information, with examples including usernames, passwords, and credit card account information, by masquerading as a trustworthy entity in an electronic communication. Phishing is typically carried out by an e-mail directing users to enter their information at the fraudster's Web site. Users of Internet services such as PayPal, eBay, and online banks are common targets.

Pretty Good Privacy (PGP): An encryption solution that is used mainly to protect e-mails. A weakness of PGP is the fact that it uses a more distributed form of certificate authentication than entities such as VeriSign. Whereas VeriSign maintains centralized control over issuing and revoking digital certificates, PGP authentication is more distributed. Any company with a PGP server can issue digital certificates. This decentralization increases the risk of fraudulent digital signatures floating around.

Privacy Screen: A removable screen that fits over your laptop monitor that is designed to blank out the screen when looked at from an angle. Many of these screens have an antiglare feature as well. Privacy screens can also reduce the amount of wear and tear of a laptop monitor, thus saving you money. A removable privacy filter is cheaper to replace than the monitor on your laptop.

Protocol: Also known as a transport protocol, a protocol is a standard (language) by which computers communicate with each other.

Removable Media: Devices that by design can be either plugged into, or inserted in, a computer and then be removed. Examples include CDs, thumb drives, iPods, and external hard drives. Removable media almost universally have the ability to have data written to them. A notable exception would a read-only CD-ROM drive.

Removable Media Encryption (RME): A software solution that can encrypt data on removable storage devices such as floppy disks, CDs, thumb drives, PDAs and more. Once attached to a computer that has RME installed on it, the host system will push the encryption onto the removable device. Any data loaded on the removable device will be encrypted at the hard drive level. This protects the confidentiality of the data if the device were to be stolen.

Router: A device used for network addressing. As data transmissions come to a router, it will determine the next path it should take from there. While not a firewall, a router can also block network communications.

Script Kiddies: A term used for to describe young, inexperienced hackers who use scripts and programs developed by others to perform their hacking attacks without themselves possessing a thorough knowledge of computing or how the programs even work. In most cases, the programs used by script kiddies are widely available on the Internet free of charge.

Service Pack: An accumulation of patches and fixes combined to make for a single large software update.

Shareware: A "try it before you buy it" type of software, with a limited free trial period. A fee is usually required to obtain a user license for use beyond the trial period.

Shoulder Surfing: The act of peering over somebody's shoulder and attempt to read what they're reading. This can include data on their computer monitor as well as printed material.

Sneaker Net: A colloquial name given to a manual form of file sharing. Sneaker net usually entailed copying data to a removable storage device such as a floppy disk, walking it over to the other computer, and loading the data on to it. Computer engineers generally known for their casual dress often wore sneakers, hence the name. This form of copying data from one workstation to another predated the advent of computer networking. Computer networking allows files to be shared over the network, without requiring data to be loaded onto a disk and physically carried from one system to the other.

Social Engineering: A term used to describe the use of a variety of social techniques aimed at tricking people to pass along their password, access code, account number, or simply to access to a computer.

Social Networking Sites: Web sites that are designed to bring groups of people together, often allowing them to create online user accounts. Many social networking sites allow users to also upload pictures, a brief (if not always honest) description of themselves, and to participate in chat rooms. Popular social networking sites include YouTube, MySpace, and Facebook.

SPIT: Short for Spam over Internet Telephony, a new kind of spam that leaves mass voice mail messages in your inbox. The result: you can be caught in a denial of service attack.

Spyware: As the name suggests, spyware is software whose primary purpose is to gather information about the system that it resides on, or the data files contained therein, without the knowledge of the use. An example of spyware is a keystroke logger that can record every keystroke a user makes. This can be used to gain access to a user's account name and password.

Surge Suppressor: A device used to protect electronic equipment from spikes in electrical power. They often double as power strips, as most models of surge suppressors can accommodate six or more devices.

Switch: Similar to a hub, a device that is used for connecting multiple devices together on a computer network. Considered to be a more "intelligent" device than a hub, as it can make routing decisions whereas a hub simply acts as a network concentrator. A switch is also capable of connecting different network segments together.

Thumb Drive: A colloquial name for what is more accurately referred to as a USB drive or a jump drive. A thumb drive fits in a computer's USB port and can store large amounts of data. Common uses include data backup or as a medium for transferring data from one computer to another.

Trojan Horse: As the mythical name suggests, a piece of a destructive program that is disguised as a legitimate piece of software. A Trojan horse may appear as a useful program, or as something of interest such as a sound file or an image file. At a high level, there are generally two types of Trojan horses. One is a legitimate piece of software that a hacker has corrupted. The other type is a program that a hacker has written himself, like an image file. Just like its ancient Greek counterpart, a computer Trojan horse needs to gain entrance to your computer system in order to function and is dependent on actions from their target users.

Uninterrupted Power Supply (UPS): Best described as an external emergency battery, and generally used to provide an alternative source of electricity in the event of a disruption in main power. UPS systems can be sized to either allow for a controlled shutdown of computers and other electrical devices such as printers, or allow them to continue to operate until main power has been restored.

Universal Serial Port (USB Port): A standard computer interface that allows peripheral devices (digital cameras, printers, MP3 players, game joysticks, keyboards, mice, etc.) to be attached to computers. The majority of thumb drives connect to computers via a USB port. Today, many keyboard and mice connect to computers using the USB port as well.

Virtual Private Network (VPN): A secure and private communications channel companies use to communicate with each other over a public network such as the Internet. VPNs also allow remote users to securely connect to their company's network. VPNs are generally protected by both a username/password as well as a separate form of authentication such as an ID/fob (token).

Virus (Computer Virus): A malicious software program that has the ability to replicate itself and to infect a computer with neither the knowledge nor the permission of the end user. The original virus is capable of making modified copies of itself, and the copies may also make changes to themselves, as is the case with what is known as a metamorphic virus. This is similar to how the flu virus that affects humans changes from year to year. A computer virus cannot spread from computer to computer by itself, but requires a delivery method to attack uninfected computers. However, this can be accomplished in many different ways. An end user can unknowingly send a computer virus to others in the form of an e-mail or as an attachment within an instant message. Computer viruses can also be spread by sharing data on removable devices such as CDs or thumb drives. Since many computers are now connected to the Internet, computer viruses can spread to a great number of systems quite quickly. Not only can a computer virus reproduce itself, but its copies can reproduce as well. In this way, their growth can be exponential in nature. Some computer viruses are malicious in nature and can damage programs, delete files, and even erase all the data on a computer hard drive. Other viruses are more of a nuisance in nature, and often reveal themselves as a "harmless" video or audio message. Even the more benign computer viruses can cause problems in the form of performance degradation. Today, there are quite literally millions of computer viruses in existence, with new ones being discovered daily.

Vishing: An attempt to fraudulently acquire sensitive information, with examples including usernames, passwords, and credit card account information, by masquerading as a trustworthy entity. Unlike phishing, which utilizes fraudulent e-mails, vishing uses the telephone to trick people into disclosing their personal information, allowing the fraudster to attempt to commit identity theft, financial fraud, or both.

VoIP: Also known as Voice over Internet Protocol, VoIP allows people to place phone calls over the Internet. VoIP works with regular telephones and requires an adaptor as well as Internet service. The faster the Internet service, the better. The service is generally cheaper for people and businesses that place a lot of calls, especially to foreign countries.

Warchalking: Marks drawn by hackers on the sidewalks outside of businesses that have wireless Internet access. The different symbols indicate not only the existence of a wireless network, but also any security controls, or lack thereof, that are being utilized. Warchalking is actually an offshoot of the old hobo marks of the Depression era, indicating places that were friendly to hobos, providing free food or even a place to sleep.

Web Mail: Internet (Web)-based e-mail, which is in contrast to desktop-based e-mail clients such as Microsoft Outlook. Common Web mail implementations include Hotmail, Yahoo Mail, Gmail and more. They are generally free of charge.

Wedge: A portable device capable of storing the information that is contained on the magnetic strips of credit cards. Wedges are used by fraudsters who will then copy the data to their computer in order to make illegal purchases with the stolen credit card information.

WiFi Protected Access (WPA and WPA-2): Two methods used to encrypt data that is transmitted over wireless computer networks. WPA-2 is the current de facto standard protocol for securely sending data over wireless networks. WPA was developed after WEP), while a new standard, which became WPA-2, was still being created. Both WPA and WPA-2 were developed when weaknesses were discovered in WEP, Wireless Equivalent Protocol. WPA-2 uses the Advanced Encryption Standard to encrypt data versus RC4, as both WEP and WPA do.

Wikipedia: Also referred to as "Wiki," Wikipedia is an Internet-based online dictionary. Unlike a Webster's Dictionary that is written by employees, the main source for Wikipedia's content is Internet users. The Wikipedia staff does try to check on the accuracy of the submissions, however.

WiMax: Short for Worldwide Interoperability for Microwave Access, a form of wireless connectivity that offers both greater range and greater speeds than more traditional wireless. WiMax can be used for connecting to computer networks as well as for cell phone connectivity.

Wired Equivalent Privacy (WEP): One of the first standards for protecting data being transmitted over a wireless network. Vulnerabilities discovered in WEP led to it being replaced by WPA and WPA-2 in 2003 and 2004, respectively. Using readily available software tools, WEP can be cracked in less than one minute. For that reason, it is no long appropriate for use in sending sensitive data over wireless networks.

Wireless: Generally refers to any type of electronic data transmission that occurs without the use of wires. This can include close-range devices such as wireless keyboards and mice. Wireless headsets for cell phones is another very common usage. In networking terms, wireless entails being able to connect a computer to a network, again without the use of any network cables (wires). Common users include Internet cafés. Many hotel rooms will also offer wireless connectivity.

Worm: A program that is self-replicating. A computer worm is also capable of sending itself to other computers on the network without any manual human intervention. Worms can cause damage by design and, if nothing else, can take up network bandwidth as they send themselves to other systems on the network. Unlike a virus, a computer worm does not need to attach itself to another program.

Zombie Computer: A computer that has been compromised by a hacker unbeknownst to its legitimate user. A "zombied" computer will function normally. It will carry out the intent of the hacker when given further instructions remotely, or at a predetermined time based on instructions included at the time the computer was compromised. Hackers generally create zombies both to hide their true identities and to increase their attack power by taking over a large number of computers.

INDEX

ABOUT THE AUTHOR

PHILIP ALEXANDER is the Director of Security Operations for a fraud-management company. Alexander holds technical as well as security certifications (CISSP, ISSMP, MCSE, MCT) and has been working in the computer field since the 1980s in both the public and private sectors. He is the author of *Information Security: A Manager's Guide to Thwarting Data Thieves and Hackers* (Praeger Security International, 2007).